A Note From Rick Renner

I am on a personal quest to see a "revival of the Bible" so people can establish their lives on a firm foundation that will stand strong and endure the test as the end-time storm winds begin to intensify.

In order to experience a revival of the Bible in your personal life, it is important to take time each day to read, receive, and apply its truths to your life. James tells us that if we will continue in the perfect law of liberty — refusing to be forgetful hearers but determined to be doers — we will be blessed in our ways. As you watch or listen to the programs in this series and work through this corresponding study guide, I trust that you will search the Scriptures and allow the Holy Spirit to help you hear something new from God's Word that applies specifically to your life. I encourage you to be a doer of the Word that He reveals to you. Whatever the cost, I assure you — it will be worth it.

> Thy words were found, and I did eat them;
> and thy word was unto me the joy and rejoicing of mine heart:
> for I am called by thy name, O Lord God of hosts.
> — Jeremiah 15:16

Your brother and friend in Jesus Christ,

Rick Renner

Unless otherwise indicated, all scripture quotations are taken from the *King James Version* of the Bible.

Scripture quotations marked (*AMP*) are taken from the *Amplified® Bible*, copyright © 2015 by The Lockman Foundation, La Habra, CA 90631. All rights reserved.

Scripture quotations marked (*AMPC*) are taken from the *Amplified® Bible, Classic Edition*. Copyright © 1954, 1958, 1962, 1964, 1965, 1987 by The Lockman Foundation. Used by permission. **www.Lockman.org**.

Scripture quotations marked (*MSG*) are taken from *The Message*, copyright © 1993, 2002, 2018 by Eugene H. Peterson. Used by permission of NavPress. All rights reserved. Represented by Tyndale House Publishers, Inc.

Scripture quotations marked (*NIV*) are taken from *Holy Bible, New International Version®, NIV®* Copyright ©1973, 1978, 1984, 2011 by Biblica, Inc.® Used by permission. All rights reserved worldwide.

Scripture quotations marked (*NKJV*) are taken from the *New King James Version®*. Copyright © 1982 by Thomas Nelson. Used by permission. All rights reserved.

Scripture quotations marked (*RIV*) are taken from *Renner Interpretive Version*. Copyright © 2021 by Rick Renner.

Scripture quotations marked (*TLB*) are taken from *The Living Bible* copyright © 1971. Used by permission of Tyndale House Publishers, Inc., Carol Stream, Illinois 60188. All rights reserved.

Last-Days Survival Guide

Copyright © 2020 by Rick Renner
1814 W. Tacoma St.
Broken Arrow, OK 74012-1406

Published by Rick Renner Ministries
www.renner.org

ISBN 13: 978-1-6675-0594-7

eBook ISBN 13: 978-1-6675-0595-4

All rights reserved. No portion of this book may be reproduced or transmitted in any form or by any means — electronic, mechanical, photocopy, recording, scanning, or other — except for brief quotations in critical reviews or articles, without the prior written permission of the Publisher.

How To Use This Study Guide

This fifteen-lesson study guide corresponds to *"Last-Days Survival Guide" with Rick Renner* (**Renner TV**). Each lesson in this study guide covers a topic that is addressed during the program series, with questions and references supplied to draw you deeper into your own private study of the Scriptures on this subject.

To derive the most benefit from this study guide, consider the following:

First, watch or listen to the program prior to working through the corresponding lesson in this guide. (Programs can also be viewed at **renner.org** by clicking on the Media/Archives links or on our Renner Ministries YouTube channel.)

Second, take the time to look up the scriptures included in each lesson. Prayerfully consider their application to your own life.

Third, use a journal or notebook to make note of your answers to each lesson's Study Questions and Practical Application challenges.

Fourth, invest specific time in prayer and in the Word of God to consult with the Holy Spirit. Write down the scriptures or insights He reveals to you.

Finally, take action! Whatever the Lord tells you to do according to His Word, do it.

For added insights on this subject, it is recommended that you obtain Rick Renner's book *Last-Days Survival Guide: A Scriptural Handbook To Prepare You for These Perilous Times*. You may also select from Rick's other available resources by placing your order at **renner.org** or by calling 1-800-742-5593.

LESSON 1

TOPIC
TAG – You're It!

SCRIPTURES
1. **2 Timothy 3:1** — This know also, that in the last days perilous times shall come.
2. **Matthew 8:28** — And when he was come to the other side into the country of the Gergesenes, there met him two possessed with devils, coming out of the tombs, exceeding fierce, so that no man might pass by that way.

GREEK WORDS
1. "this" — τοῦτο (*touto*): this; very specific
2. "also" — δέ (*de*): also; indeed; emphatically
3. "know" — γινώσκω (*ginosko*): to know something definitely, emphatically, and with absolute certainty
4. "that" — ὅτι (*hoti*): points to a specific and important point
5. "last" — ἔσχατος (*eschatos*): the ultimate end of a thing; the extreme end; used in classical Greek literature to depict a place furthest away, such as the very ends of the earth; the final port or last stopping off for a journey; something that is final; the very end
6. "perilous" — χαλεπός (*chalepos*): dangerous, risky, hurtful; pictures something that is wounding; used in literature to depict wild, vicious, uncontrollable animals that were unpredictable and dangerous; pictures a deadly menace; denotes anything that is treacherous or potentially hurtful; used to describe ugly words that when spoken are hurtful and emotionally hard to bear; carries the idea of an action, place, person, or thing that is harsh, harmful, and filled with high risk; used in Matthew 8:28 to describe the demonized men of the Gadarenes
7. "times" — καιρός (*kairos*): plural, "times"; a specific or definite season
8. "shall come" — ἐνίστημι (*enistemi*): a compound of ἐν (*en*) and ἵστημι (*histemi*); the word ἐν (*en*) means in; the word ἵστημι (*histemi*)

means to stand; to stand in; to stand in the middle of; to be surrounded; to be encumbered; to stand in the very middle of whatever is being discussed
9. "exceedingly fierce" — χαλεπός (*chalepos*): dangerous, risky, hurtful; pictures something that is wounding; used in literature to depict wild, vicious, uncontrollable animals that were unpredictable and dangerous; pictures a deadly menace; denotes anything that is treacherous or potentially hurtful; used to describe ugly words that when spoken are hurtful and emotionally hard to bear; carries the idea of an action, place, person, or thing that is harsh, harmful, and filled with high risk
10. "way" — ὁδός (*hodos*): road; way

SYNOPSIS

The 15 lessons in this study guide titled, ***Last-Days Survival Guide*** will focus on the following topics:

- TAG — You're It!
- 25 Signs of the Last Days
- The Leaning Tower of Pisa
- Snooty Agenda-Setters
- An Evil Last-Days Agenda
- A World Full of Ingrates
- The Dark Connection Between Unthankfulness and Unholiness
- The Breakdown of Family and Relationship
- Widespread Violence
- An End-Times Hurricane
- Pandemics, Hedonism, and Spiritual Mannequins
- Creeps!
- Reprobates!
- A Hidden Prophecy!
- How To Navigate an End-Times Storm

When you were growing up, did you ever play tag with your neighborhood friends? It's a timeless game in which one person is "it," and his task is to feverishly run around trying to tag another person, making that individual "it." Most people prefer to be the "tag-*er*" rather than the "tag-*ee*."

If we take the concept of this game and apply it to those living in the world, at some point in history, a generation will arise that will be the final generation to live at the end of the age. Looking at the numerous last-days signs all converging on the world scene, it seems as though the Holy Spirit has reached out and touched our generation and said, *"TAG! You're it!* You're the generation to live at the end of the age on the prophetic calendar."

The good news is, not only has God tagged us, but He has also anointed us to live successfully in these final hours. He has equipped us with His Word, the power of the Holy Spirit, the blood of Jesus, and the name of Jesus — and through Him, we can do everything we need to do to thrive in these *last* of the last days!

The emphasis of this lesson:

The Holy Spirit has urgently alerted us that in the last of the last days, we will be surrounded on all sides by times that are dangerous, risky, and menacing. Yet we are not to be afraid — rather, we are to boldly walk in Christ's authority, bringing hope, healing, and freedom to the people and places around us.

Every Single Word Is Important!

Writing under the inspiration of the Holy Spirit, Paul prophetically told us what would take place at the end of the age. Specifically, in Second Timothy 3:1, he said, "This know also, that in the last days perilous times shall come." What's very interesting about this passage is that every word carries great meaning and importance.

First is the word "this," which is the Greek word *touto*, and it describes *something very specific*. It is as if the Holy Spirit is raising His voice and emphatically saying, "*This, this, this!*" The next word is "also," which is the Greek word *de*, and it means *also; indeed;* or *emphatically*. This word *de* is like an exclamation mark, and by using it, the Holy Spirit is sounding an alarm, urging us to *emphatically* and *categorically* "know" something.

This brings us to the word "know," which is a form of the Greek word *ginosko*, and it means *to know something definitely, emphatically, and with absolute certainty.* The use of this word denotes the Holy Spirit's adamancy — that He is not telling us something that *might* happen or that *could possibly* develop. Rather, He is about to describe something that emphatically and most definitely will take place in the end of the age. So when we read, "This know also," it is the equivalent of saying, "This is something so urgent and absolutely certain that *it must be known, must be recognized,* and *must be acknowledged.*"

Then Paul adds the word "that" — the Greek word *hoti* — which is a "pointer word," because it points to a specific and important point. It is the equivalent of saying, "Here is exactly what you need to know." He then adds, "…That in the last days perilous times shall come" (2 Timothy 3:1).

What Does 'in the Last Days' Mean?

In the original Greek, the phrase "in the last days" is *en eschatais hemeras.* The word *en* means *to be in* or *to be inside of something,* and the word *hemeras* is the Greek word for *days.* This brings us to the word *eschatais* — translated here as "last." It is the plural form of the word *eschatos,* and it is where we get the word "eschatology," which is *the study of the end times or last things.* Throughout the New Testament, this word is used to describe *the ultimate end of a thing* or *the extreme end.* In classical Greek literature, it was used to depict *a place furthest away, such as the very ends of the earth.*

In a navigational sense, this word denoted *the final port* or *last stopping-off point for a journey.* Although a ship in transit stops at many points on the route to its destination, the word *eschatas* depicts *the very last port, the last stopping off point.* When you have reached the *"eschatos,"* you've reached the end of the road, and the journey is finished.

Now if we stop here and look at the original Greek meaning of the first eight words of Second Timothy 3:1, we could literally translate it, "This emphatically know — you must know it, you must embrace it, and you must understand it because it is most certainly going to happen. Specifically, that in the timeframe called the 'last days' — when you've sailed to the end of the Church age, when you've reached the final port and there's nowhere else to go.…" What's going to take place when we come to the very end? Paul prophesied, "…Perilous times shall come" (2 Timothy 3:1).

The Last-Days Generation Will Be *Surrounded on All Sides* by Difficulty

Interestingly, when you read the last part of this verse in Greek, it says, "shall come times perilous." In Greek, the phrase "shall come" is a translation of the word *enistemi*, which is a compound of the words *en* and *histemi*. Again, the word *en* means *in* or *to be inside of something*, and the word *histemi* means *to stand*.

When these words are compounded to form *enistemi*, it means *to stand in, to stand in the middle of, to be surrounded*, or *to be encumbered by*. It carries the idea of standing in the very middle of whatever is being discussed with the feeling that it cannot be avoided or escaped. It is a picture of one who is so encompassed by something that there seems to be no way out.

By using the word *enistemi* ("shall come"), the Holy Spirit prophetically declares that those who live in the very last season of the age will feel as if they're positioned in the very midst of, surrounded by, and encumbered on every side by unavoidable developments. This last-days generation will feel like they are being assaulted by *perilous times* and that there is no escaping from what is standing all around them.

What Are 'Perilous Times'?

This brings us to the phrase "perilous times." The word "times" is the Greek word *kairoi*, which is the plural form of *kairos*, and it describes *seasons, times*, or *a specific, definite season*. It also denotes *an opportunity*, which means when we've sailed to the end of the age, there will be *times* or *opportunities* for perilous things to take place. Rather than prophesying just a single event, Paul is forecasting a plethora of *perilous* things occurring.

In Greek, the word "perilous" is *chalepos*, a rare word used only twice in the New Testament. It means *dangerous, risky, or hurtful*, and it pictures *something that is wounding*. It is a word used in literature to depict *wild, vicious, uncontrollable animals that were unpredictable and dangerous*. This word *chalepos* can also picture *a deadly menace* or denote *anything that is treacherous or potentially hurtful*. It has also been used to describe *ugly words that when spoken are hurtful and emotionally hard to bear*. It carries the idea of *an action, place, person, or thing that is harsh, harmful, and filled with high risk*.

In addition to Second Timothy 3:1, the word *chalepos* is also used in Matthew 8:28. Here, Jesus and His disciples had just finished crossing the Sea of Galilee when something unexpected confronted them. The Bible says, "And when he was come to the other side into the country of the Gergesenes, there met him two possessed with devils, coming out of the tombs, exceeding fierce, so that no man might pass by that way."

In this verse, the phrase "exceeding fierce" is the Greek word *chalepos*. Again, it describes *something dangerous*, *risky*, or *hurtful*. This tells us that these demonized men were *menacing* and posed a great *danger* to anyone who came near them. If a person ventured to pass by that "way," his or her life was at *risk* of being *hurt* or *wounded* by the evil spirits operating through these men.

The word "way" is the Greek word *hodos*, which describes a *road*. Very near to where the demoniacs lived, there was an ancient road that ran along the Sea of Galilee, allowing people to travel north and south. However, because of the terrorizing presence of the demonized men, the people became terrified of taking the road (*hodos*) for fear of the potential dangers they might encounter. Hence, the evil spirits working through these men created an *impasse* that people just couldn't seem to get around.

Deal With These Last Days Just as Jesus Dealt with the Demoniacs

Taking this idea and applying it to Paul's words in Second Timothy 3:1, we find that when we come to the very end of the age, there are going to be many seasons or opportunities that will create an impasse for those who are living during that time. People will be surrounded and encumbered on every side by *chalepos kairoi* — "perilous times." Event after event will feel dangerous, risky, and menacing — just like the presence of the demon-possessed men in Jesus' day.

Ironically, what terrified others compelled Jesus to action. Immediately upon reaching the shore of the Gergesenes, Jesus came forward and cast the demons out of the men and set the region free. What had previously been an impasse due to vicious and treacherous conditions became a wide-open roadway for all to travel freely. Life changed for everyone because Jesus came on the scene!

The way Jesus dealt with the impasse of His day is the way we are to deal with the impasses of these last days. Rather than stay in our homes, close the blinds, and hide, *we must refuse to allow fear to grip our hearts!* Instead of cowering in fear, we are called to use the authority Christ gave us and bring deliverance, freedom, and peace to people and places where the devil has tried to bring chaos, hazard, and hurt.

Taking into account the original Greek meaning, here is the *Renner Interpretive Version* (*RIV*) of Second Timothy 3:1:

> **You emphatically and categorically need to know with unquestionable certainty that in the very end of days — when time has sailed to its last port and no more time remains for the journey — that last season will stand in the midst of uncontrollable, unpredictable, hurtful, treacherous, and menacing times that will be emotionally difficult for people to bear.**

Realize that God loves us, and He is not telling us this to *scare* us, but to *prepare* us for the treacherous and menacing times in which we live. He has given us the indwelling Holy Spirit, the name of Jesus, the blood of Jesus, as well as all the promises of His Word. If we use these powerful tools, we will sail through these last days victoriously.

Remember, Jesus Is Coming To Get Us!

Many ask the question, "Is the word 'rapture' in the Bible? The word "rapture" is actually a translation of the Latin word *raptura*, and in Greek, it's the word *harpadzō*, which means *to snatch out of danger just in the nick of time*. Although the word "rapture" itself is not found in the English New Testament, the word *harpadzō* is, and we find it in **First Thessalonians 4:17** where the apostle Paul is describing the *catching away* of believers who are living on the earth when Christ returns. Paul says:

> **Then we which are alive and remain shall be caught up together with them in the clouds, to meet the Lord in the air: and so shall we ever be with the Lord.**

The words "caught up" in this verse are a translation of the Greek word *harpadzō*. So while the English word "rapture" itself doesn't appear in the New Testament text, the words "caught up" do, and they explicitly describe the rapture — that indescribable moment when Jesus comes for His Church. Scripture says that in the twinkling of an eye, the dead in Christ are going to be raised first, and all believers who are alive and awaiting His return will be caught up (*harpadzo*) to meet the Lord in the air to be with Him forever!

STUDY QUESTIONS

> Study to shew thyself approved unto God, a workman that needeth not to be ashamed, rightly dividing the word of truth.
> — 2 Timothy 2:15

1. From your personal observation of watching and listening to the news, how would you describe the condition of the world? Your country? What alarms you most?
2. Why do you think the Holy Spirit so emphatically and urgently communicated the condition of society in the last of the last days?
3. Carefully read what the Holy Spirit moved the apostle Paul to write in Acts 17:24-28. What does this tell you personally about your life and the lives of others? (Also consider Psalm 139:13-16.)

PRACTICAL APPLICATION

> But be ye doers of the word, and not hearers only, deceiving your own selves.
> — James 1:22

1. In your own words, describe the meaning of the words "last days." Likewise, briefly explain what is meant by the phrase "perilous times."
2. What "perilous" circumstances have you personally had to navigate? What harsh, unpredictable situations are you currently standing in the middle of that seem to surround you on all sides? Take time to meditate on this amazing promise and share how it encourages your faith.

> "…For He [God] **Himself has said, I will not in any way fail you nor give you up nor leave you without support.** [I will] **not,** [I will] **not,** [I will] **not in any degree leave you helpless nor forsake nor let** [you] **down (relax My hold on you)!** [Assuredly not!] **So we take comfort and are encouraged and confidently and boldly say, The Lord is my Helper; I will not be seized with alarm** [I will not fear or dread or be terrified]. **What can man do to me?**
> — **Hebrews 13:5,6 (*AMPC*)**

LESSON 2

TOPIC
25 Signs of the Last Days

SCRIPTURES
2 Timothy 3:1-9, 13 — This know also, that in the last days perilous times shall come. For men shall be lovers of their own selves, covetous, boasters, proud, blasphemers, disobedient to parents, unthankful, unholy, without natural affection, trucebreakers, false accusers, incontinent, fierce, despisers of those that are good, traitors, heady, highminded, lovers of pleasures more than lovers of God; having a form of godliness, but denying the power thereof: from such turn away. For of this sort are they which creep into houses, and lead captive silly women laden with sins, led away with divers lusts, ever learning, and never able to come to the knowledge of the truth. Now as Jannes and Jambres withstood Moses, so do these also resist the truth: men of corrupt minds, reprobate concerning the faith. But they shall proceed no further: for their folly shall be manifest unto all men, as theirs also was. …But evil men and seducers shall wax worse and worse, deceiving, and being deceived.

GREEK WORDS
1. "know" — γινώσκω (*ginosko*): to know something definitely, emphatically, and with absolute certainty
2. "that" — ὅτι (*hoti*): points to a specific and important point
3. "last" — ἔσχατος (*eschatos*): the ultimate end of a thing; the extreme end; used in classical Greek literature to depict a place furthest away, such as the very ends of the earth; the final port or last stopping off for a journey; something that is final; the very end
4. "perilous" — χαλεπός (*chalepos*): dangerous, risky, hurtful; pictures something that is wounding; used in literature to depict wild, vicious, uncontrollable animals that were unpredictable and dangerous; pictures a deadly menace; denotes anything that is treacherous or potentially hurtful; used to describe ugly words that when spoken are hurtful and emotionally hard to bear; carries the idea of an action, place, person, or thing that is harsh, harmful, and filled with high

risk; used in Matthew 8:28 to describe the demonized men of the Gadarenes
5. "times" — καιρός (*kairos*): plural, "times"; a specific or definite season
6. "shall come" — ἐνίστημι (*enistemi*): a compound of ἐν (*en*) and ἵστημι (*histemi*); the word ἐν (*en*) means in; the word ἵστημι (*histemi*) means to stand; compounded, it means to stand in; to stand in the middle of; to be surrounded; to be encumbered; to stand in the very middle of whatever is being discussed
7. "lovers of their own selves" — φίλαυτος (*philautos*): from φίλος (*philos*) and αὐτός (*autos*); the word φίλος (*philos*) means to love or to be fond of, and it denotes the love, fondness, attraction, or romantic feelings one has for another; the word αὐτός (*autos*) means oneself; when compounded, it means love of self and actually describes inordinate self-love, self-preoccupation, or one in love with and consumed with himself; self-absorbed; self-focused; inordinate self-love

SYNOPSIS

When Paul wrote his second letter to Timothy, Timothy was living in Ephesus and serving as the pastor of the church at Ephesus. At that time, Timothy was already dealing with challenging societal issues and problems that had made their way into the Church. Under the anointing of the Holy Spirit, the apostle Paul exhorted Timothy and at the same time pointed nearly 2,000 years into the future to describe what would occur at the very end of the Church age.

In Second Timothy 3:2-13, Paul cited 25 specific signs we will see that will confirm that we have reached the last of the last days. Again, the Holy Spirit doesn't give us this information to *scare* us, but to *prepare* us to make the most of the times in which we live.

The emphasis of this lesson:

Through Paul, the Holy Spirit described 25 characteristics that will emerge in society at the very end of the age. The chief sign that we've entered the last of the last days is that society will be consumed with an inordinate, unhealthy love of self. As a result, everything else will become off-balance.

The Holy Spirit Emphatically Urged Us To Know and Comprehend Something

Without question, every word in Scripture carries great weight and importance — including the words in Second Timothy 3:1, which says: "This know also, that in the last days perilous times shall come." As we saw in our first lesson, the meaning of each word in this verse tells us something unique that the Holy Spirit wants us to understand about the last of the last days.

First, we noted that the word "this" is the Greek word *touto*, and it is pointing to *something very specific*. The next word "also" is the Greek word *de*. It signifies *something indeed*, *something categorical*, or *something emphatic*. It is like an exclamation mark, saying, "This! This specifically!" Paul then added the word "know," which is the Greek word *ginoske*, a direct form of *ginosko*, meaning *to know something definitely*, *emphatically*, and *with absolute certainty*.

Through the combined use of these three words, it is as if the Holy Spirit is raising His voice and reaching through the pages of Scripture and telling us, "You need to know this emphatically; this is something you must acknowledge, you must comprehend, and you must embrace." The next word is "that," the Greek word *hoti*, which is a "pointer word" that points to *a specific and important point*. It is used to focus the reader's attention and is the equivalent of saying, "You must know and must comprehend exactly that…."

'In the Last Days…'

We saw that the word "in" is the little Greek word *en*, and it means *in*, like *to be inside a time frame*. Specifically, Paul was talking about being *in* the "last days," which in Greek is *eschateis hemeras*. The word *eschateis* is the plural form of *eschatos* and is where we get the word "eschatology," which is *the study of end times*. The word *eschatos* describes *the very ultimate end of a thing*. It was also a seafaring term used to describe a ship that had sailed to the last port, and there were no stopping points after it.

Hence, the word *eschatos* could describe the very last day of the week, the very last day of the month, or the very last day of the year. But it would only describe *the very last one* or *the ultimate end* of each one. In Second Timothy 3:1, Paul used this word to describe the very last of the last days.

The word "days" here is the Greek word *hemeras*, which is plural for *days*. So when Paul said, "in the last days," he was saying, *"In the time frame of the ultimate end of the age — when time has sailed to its very last port, and no more time remains on the journey. It is during that very last of the last days…*

'Perilous Times Shall Come'

Now the word order of this portion of Scripture in Greek actually says, "shall come times perilous." The words "shall come" are a translation of the Greek word *enistemi*, which is a compound of the words *en* and *histemi*. Again, the word *en* means *to be in* or *to be inside of something*, and the word *histemi* means *to stand*. When these words are compounded to form the new word *enistemi*, it means *to stand in; to stand in the middle of; to be surrounded by;* or *to be encumbered with*. It depicts someone surrounded on every side, standing in the very middle of whatever is being discussed.

By using this word, the Holy Spirit is telling us that when we've sailed to the very end of the age, we will know it, because we will suddenly feel like we're stuck in the middle of, and we're surrounded and encumbered by, *perilous times* that appear to be inescapable.

In Greek, the word "times" is *kairoi*, which is plural and from the word *kairos*. It describes *times, seasons,* or even *opportunities*. When we insert this meaning into Second Timothy 3:1, we understand that when we reach the very last of the last days and time has come to an end, those who are living in that period will feel as though they are stuck smack dab in the middle of *times, seasons,* and *opportunities* that are "perilous" — which is the Greek word *chalepoi*.

The word *chalepoi* is the plural form of *chalepos*, and it describes *something dangerous, risky,* or *hurtful*. It pictures *something that is wounding* and is a word used in ancient Greek literature to depict *wild, vicious, uncontrollable animals that were unpredictable and dangerous*. It also pictures *a deadly menace* and denotes *anything that is treacherous or potentially hurtful*. It carries the idea of *an action, place, person, or thing that is harsh, harmful, and filled with high risk*. We saw in Lesson 1 that the only other place the word *chalepos* is used is in Matthew 8:28, and it described the demonized men of the Gadarenes who were "exceeding fierce."

When we insert the meaning of *chalepoi* into Second Timothy 3:1, we see the Holy Spirit telling us through Paul that those of us who are living at the end of the age are going to feel like we're surrounded and encumbered on all sides by dangerous, menacing, and uncontrollable times that appear to be inescapable. These treacherous opportunities will be in front of us, behind us, and alongside us.

When Did the 'Last Days' Begin?

Now, maybe you've heard someone say, "People have been saying for the last 2,000 years that we're living in the last days and Jesus is coming back soon. How is today any different than the days before it?"

The truth is, the last days *did* begin just after Christ ascended into Heaven and the Church was birthed on the earth! When the Holy Spirit was poured out on the Day of Pentecost and Peter stood up to preach, he quoted from Joel 2:28 saying, "…This is that which was spoken by the prophet Joel; And it shall come to pass *in the last days*, saith God, I will pour out of my Spirit upon all flesh…" (Acts 2:16,17). When Peter made this declaration, he was declaring that the outpouring of the Holy Spirit on the Day of Pentecost officially triggered the beginning of the last days.

Thus, the reality is, we *have* been living in the last days for nearly 2,000 years, and the last days will continue right up until the day of the rapture of the Church. The Rapture — or "catching away" of believers — will trigger the beginning of the Great Tribulation.

To be clear, the last 2,000 years and the present time are also referred to as *the age of grace* or *the Church age*. Both classifications are true — we are living in *the Church age*, also known as *the age of grace*. At the same time, biblically speaking, these last 2,000 years of history are also called *the last days*, and they began on the Day of Pentecost.

Now, when we come to Second Timothy 3:1, Paul was *not* talking about the beginning or even the middle of the last days. His Spirit-led choice of words tells us that he was specifically prophesying about the very end of this period. He said, "When you come to the ultimate end of the Church age — at the very edge of time, just before Jesus returns, when you've reached the final port and can't go any further — in those last of the last days, perilous times shall come." This informs us that the very end of the age is going to be unique. Something is going to happen that's different than anything that has happened in the rest of that age.

25 Characteristics of the Last-Days Society

What specifically will these perilous times look like? The apostle Paul — continuing to write under the anointing of the Holy Spirit — gave us 25 signs or characteristics of the last of the last days in Second Timothy 3:2-13. These descriptions include those who exhibit the following characteristics:

In 2 Timothy 3:2, we find…

1. Lovers of their own selves

2. Covetous

3. Boasters

4. Proud

5. Blasphemers

6. Disobedient to parents

7. Unthankful

8. Unholy

In 2 Timothy 3:3, we find…

9. Without natural affection

10. Trucebreakers

11. False accusers

12. Incontinent

13. Fierce

14. Despisers of those that are good

In 2 Timothy 3:4, we find…

15. Traitors

16. Heady

17. High-minded

18. Lovers of pleasures more than lovers of God

In 2 Timothy 3:5, we find…

19. Have a form of godliness

20. But deny the power thereof

In 2 Timothy 3:6,7, we find…

21. Creep into houses

22. Lead captive "silly women laden with sins and led away with divers lusts — ever learning, and never able to come to the knowledge of the truth"

In 2 Timothy 3:8, we find…

23. Those who are like Jannes and Jambres who withstood Moses and resisted the truth

24. Men of corrupt minds and reprobate concerning the faith

In 2 Timothy 3:13, we find…

25. Evil men and seducers that shall wax worse and worse, deceiving, and being deceived

We will cover each of these 25 characteristics in more depth in the lessons that follow. For the remainder of this lesson, we will focus on the primary sign of the last-days society, which is found at the beginning of Second Timothy 3:2.

'Men Shall Be Lovers of Their Own Selves' and All of Society Will Be Affected

In Second Timothy 3:2, Paul wrote, "For men shall be lovers of their own selves…." The phrase "lovers of their own selves" is the bizarre Greek word *philautoi*, which is the plural form of *philautos*. This is a compound of the words *philos* and *autos*. The word *philos* means *to love or to be fond of*, and it denotes *the love, fondness, attraction,* or *romantic feelings one has for another*. And the word *autos* describes *oneself*. When we compound these two words, it means *love of self* and describes *inordinate self-love, self-preoccupation*, or *one in love with and consumed with himself*. It presents the idea of one who is *self-focused, self-centered,* and *self-absorbed*.

Here, the Holy Spirit alerts us that the chief sign that we've entered the last of the last days is that society will be consumed with a love of self (*philautos*). Their focus and love will be primarily directed toward themselves, which means society will become narcissistic, self-consumed, off-balance, and faulty at the core.

As we noted, the Greek word *philautoi* is plural, which implies this characteristic will be widespread and prominent in the last of the last days. It not only refers to individuals, but the whole of society. Out of this flawed foundation of self-love, the culture will drift further and further off track.

Of course, there's nothing wrong with loving ourselves. Jesus told us in Matthew 22:39 that we're to love our neighbor as we love ourselves. But Paul's words in Second Timothy 3:2 were not talking about healthy love — they were warning against a love that is narcissistic, self-consumed, self-obsessed, and thinking of self above everything else.

Friend, since we know this is going to occur at the end of the age, we need to listen to what the Holy Spirit is saying and make sure that we're not a part of the *philautos* crowd — by keeping our love directed in the right place. Our affection needs to be directed toward the Lord first and then toward others. As you maintain a servant's heart toward God and those He's placed around you, you will be protected from being infected by the narcissistic, self-consumed mind-set that is "going viral" in these last days.

Taking into account the original Greek meaning, here again is the *Renner Interpretive Version* (*RIV*) of 2 Timothy 3:1.

> **You emphatically and categorically need to know with unquestionable certainty that in the very end of days — when time has sailed to its last port and no more time remains for the journey — that last season will stand in the midst of uncontrollable, unpredictable, hurtful, treacherous, and menacing times that will be emotionally difficult for people to bear.**

When Is the Rapture Going To Take Place?

According to Scripture, the Rapture is going to occur at the end of the Church age. Acts 2 reveals that the Church age began on the Day of Pentecost, when God poured His Spirit out on believers. At the end of the Church age, Jesus will return to rapture the Church. We read about it in **First Thessalonians 4:16,17:**

> **For the Lord himself shall descend from heaven with a shout, with the voice of the archangel, and with the trump of God: and the dead in Christ shall rise first:**
>
> **Then we which are alive and remain shall be caught up together with them in the clouds, to meet the Lord in the air: and so shall we ever be with the Lord.**

Again, this *catching away* of the Church will take place at the very end of the Church age, and when it does, it will trigger the moment when the Great Tribulation begins.

STUDY QUESTIONS

> Study to shew thyself approved unto God, a workman that needeth not to be ashamed, rightly dividing the word of truth.
> — 2 Timothy 2:15

1. History reveals that throngs of people in the ancient city of Ephesus were captivated and obsessed with *entertainment*. Gladiator fights, chariot races, wild-animal matches, and the execution of criminals were attended by up to 30,000 people daily. What similarities or parallels can you identify between the people of Ephesus and people in our culture today?
2. The Bible tells us that in the last days, men and women will be *lovers of themselves*. What did Jesus say in Matthew 22:37-39 is the first and greatest commandment, and what is the second one like it? Write out this passage, making it your personal declaration.

PRACTICAL APPLICATION

> But be ye doers of the word, and not hearers only, deceiving your own selves.
> — James 1:22

1. The Holy Spirit foretells that people at the end of this age will be self-absorbed and self-consumed — preoccupied with meeting their own needs above anything else. After reading this lesson, do you see that you have subconsciously fallen into this narcissistic trap of *misdirected love*? If so, in what ways?

2. Take a moment and repent of any selfishness in your life. Ask the Lord to forgive you and help you cultivate the selfless heart of Jesus. (Consider Philippians 2:3-8.)
3. List at least one practical thing you can begin doing daily to focus your energy on: (a) putting God's will first; and (b) meeting the needs of others second (considering those in your family and immediate sphere of influence).

LESSON 3

TOPIC

The Leaning Tower of Pisa

SCRIPTURES

2 Timothy 3:1,2 — This know also, that in the last days perilous times shall come. For men shall be lovers of their own selves, covetous....

GREEK WORDS

1. "know" — γινώσκω (*ginosko*): to know something definitely, emphatically, and with absolute certainty
2. "last" — ἔσχατος (*eschatos*): the ultimate end of a thing; the extreme end; used in classical Greek literature to depict a place furthest away, such as the very ends of the earth; the final port or last stopping-off point for a journey; something that is final; the very end
3. "perilous" — χαλεπός (*chalepos*): dangerous, risky, hurtful; pictures something that is wounding; used in literature to depict wild, vicious, uncontrollable animals that were unpredictable and dangerous; pictures a deadly menace; denotes anything that is treacherous or potentially hurtful; used to describe ugly words that when spoken are hurtful and emotionally hard to bear; carries the idea of an action, place, person, or thing that is harsh, harmful, and filled with high risk; used in Matthew 8:28 to describe the demonized men of the Gadarenes
4. "times" — καιροί (*kairoi*): plural, "times"; a specific or definite season

5. "shall come" — ἐνίστημι (*enistemi*): a compound of ἐν (*en*) and ἵστημι (*histemi*); the word ἐν (*en*) means in; the word ἵστημι (*histemi*) means to stand; when compounded, it means to stand in; to stand in the middle of; to be surrounded; to be encumbered; to stand in the very middle of whatever is being discussed

6. "lovers of their own selves" — φίλαυτος (*philautos*): from φίλος (*philos*) and αὐτός (*autos*); the word φίλος (*philos*) means to love or to be fond of, and it denotes the love, fondness, attraction, or romantic feelings one has for another; the word αὐτός (*autos*) means oneself; when compounded, it means love of self and actually describes inordinate self-love, self-preoccupation, or one in love with and consumed with himself; self-absorbed; self-focused; inordinate self-love

7. "coveteous" — φιλάργυρος (*philarguros*): from φίλος (*philos*) and ἄργυρος (*arguros*); the word φίλος (*philos*) refers to love, fondness, attraction, and romance; the word ἄργυρος (*arguros*) is the word for silver or money; when compounded, it depicts an inordinate love of or an abnormal preoccupation with money or material possessions

SYNOPSIS

In the city of Pisa, Italy, there is a tower, which is famously called the Leaning Tower of Pisa. It is the freestanding bell tower of Pisa Cathedral. Construction of this building began in 1173, but by the year 1178, as they were continuing to build, it became obvious there was something wrong because the tower began to lean. Strangely, rather than fix the foundation, the workers tried to adjust the building to compensate for the lean, but it didn't work. It kept leaning further and further.

At different times during the centuries that followed, engineers attempted to correct the sinking problem. Although they had some success, they were never able to fully fix the tower's faulty foundation.

In many ways, society today is much like the Leaning Tower of Pisa. Although many can clearly see our foundation is flawed, they keep building on it in various ways, hoping to correct the problems. Yet we continue to teeter and sink in the wrong direction. Through the apostle Paul, the Holy Spirit warns us of how warped the world will be in the last days. If we listen to what the Spirit is saying, we can self-correct and make sure we personally build our lives on the solid foundation of His Word.

The emphasis of this lesson:

Paul prophesied that because of the proliferation of unhealthy, inordinate self-love in society, covetousness would emerge and begin to flourish at the very end of the age. This "covetousness" is an inordinate love of or an abnormal preoccupation with money or material possessions.

A Review of Our Anchor Verse
2 Timothy 3:1

Turning our attention once more to Second Timothy 3:1, we read, "This know also, that in the last days perilous times shall come." We have seen that the word **"know"** is a form of the Greek word *ginosko*, and it means *to know something definitely, emphatically, and with absolute certainty.* When the Bible says, "This know also," it's like the Holy Spirit is reaching through the pages of Scripture to grab hold of us and shake us up. With a sense of urgency, He's telling us, *"You must know this; you must acknowledge this; you must comprehend this…."*

Then Paul added the word **"that,"** which in Greek is the little word *hoti*. Essentially, this is a pointer word pointing to something very specific. In this case, it is explicitly pointing to the fact that *in the last days, perilous times shall come.*

We've also noted that the word **"last"** is a form of the Greek word *eschatos*, which describes *the ultimate end of a thing* or *the extreme end*. It is a term used in classical Greek literature to depict *a place furthest away, such as the very ends of the earth*. In the world of navigation, it was also employed to describe *the final port* or *last stopping-off point on a journey*. It is *something that is final; the very end.*

Biblically speaking, the last days began on the Day of Pentecost when Peter stood up to preach and said, "…This is that which was spoken by the prophet Joel; And it shall come to pass *in the last days*, saith God, I will pour out of my Spirit upon all flesh…" (Acts 2:16,17). This prophetic declaration marked the beginning of the last days. Thus, for the last 2,000 years, we have been living in the last days — a period that is also referred to as *the age of grace* and *the Church age*. This era will conclude the moment Jesus returns to rapture the Church.

When Paul talked about the last days in Second Timothy 3:1, he was specifically referring to the very end of this period. Essentially, he prophesied,

"When you come to the ultimate end of the Church age — at the very edge of time, when you've reached the final port and can sail no further — in those last of the last days, perilous times shall come."

The word **"perilous"** is from the Greek word *chalepos*, which describes *something dangerous*, *risky*, or *hurtful*. It pictures *something that is wounding* and is a word used in literature to depict *wild, vicious, uncontrollable animals that were unpredictable and dangerous*. It can also depict *a deadly menace* and denotes *anything that is treacherous or potentially hurtful*. Moreover, the word *chalepos* was used to describe *ugly words that when spoken are hurtful and emotionally hard to bear*. It carries the idea of an action, place, person, or thing that is harsh, harmful, and filled with high risk.

Taking into account the original Greek meaning, here is the *Renner Interpretive Version* (*RIV*) of Second Timothy 3:1.

> **You emphatically and categorically need to know with unquestionable certainty that in the very end of days — when time has sailed to its last port and no more time remains for the journey — that last season will stand in the midst of uncontrollable, unpredictable, hurtful, treacherous, and menacing times that will be emotionally difficult for people to bear.**

Isn't it amazing how accurate the Holy Spirit was in His prophetic description? He summed up our society today in every way, proving that He is all-knowing and deserving of our trust!

The Last Generation Is the 'I Am' Generation

In Second Timothy 3:2, Paul began to unpack the characteristics of the last-days culture by saying, "For men shall be lovers of their own selves...." In the original Greek language, this verse reads:

> *"Esontai gar hoi anthropoi philautoi...."*

The Greek word *esontai* means *will be*, and it is from the word *eimi*, which means *I am*. This is important to the context of this passage, as it seems to indicate that at the end of the age, we will enter into the "I am" generation — when people will be self-focused, self-obsessed, and narcissistic.

Next is the conjunction *gar*, which is translated here as the word "for" and connects us to the previous verse. Its use indicates that what Paul was about to say was a part of the perilous times that are coming. The Holy Spirit emphatically declares that in the final days of the age, people will become *esontai* (from *eimi*, meaning "I am") — they will be *self-centered, self-absorbed*, and altogether *selfish*.

Then we see the words *hoi anthropoi*, from the word *anthropos*, which describes *mankind at large*. The tense is plural, signifying that this problem will be widespread. Hence, mankind at large will become *philautoi* — a word that is a combination of the Greek words *phileo* and *autoi*. The word *phileo* means *"I love,"* and it carries the idea of *affection* and *deep devotion*. It is from the word *phil*, meaning *to love* or *to be fond of*, and it denotes *the love, fondness, attraction, or romantic feelings one has for another*. Normally, this is not a word you would use in reference to yourself, but it is a word used to describe what you feel about someone else. The word *autoi*, which is plural, is from the word *autos*, the word for *oneself*.

When these two words are compounded to form the phrase "lovers of their own selves" — the Greek word *philautos* — we get a word that means *love of self* and describes *inordinate self-love, self-preoccupation*, or *one in love with and consumed with himself*. It pictures one who is *self-absorbed or self-focused*; an *inordinate self-love*.

Misdirected Love Makes Everything Else Go Astray

Paul began this last-days list with the word *philautos* to let us know that there will be a gross misdirection and misuse of love at the end of the age. The use of the words "lovers of their own selves" — the Greek word *philautoi* — suggests what is fundamentally wrong with these people is that their love is misdirected to *self* rather than to others as was intended. This misdirection puts *self* above all others — and when *self* is made the central focus of one's life, everything else goes astray.

By saying, "For men shall be lovers of their own selves," the Holy Spirit is foretelling that people at the very end of the age will be loyal to themselves above everyone else. Their chief loyalty will *not* be to God, to their nation, to their family, to their friends, or to their employer or employees. This self-consumed, last-days society will be populated with people who are primarily devoted to *themselves* and whose lives are consequently and fundamentally lopsided and off-balance, like the Tower of Pisa.

Society Will Be 'Covetous'

Out of an unhealthy, inordinate self-love, Paul prophesied that society will also be "covetous" (*see* Second Timothy 3:2). This is a translation of the Greek word *philarguros*, which is from the words *phileo* and *arguros* — two words you would not expect to find used together. The word *phileo* means *to love* or *to be fond of* and denotes the *fondness, attraction,* and *romance* one would have or feel for another.

The second part of the word is *arguros*, which is the Greek word for *silver* or *money* and can also refer to *material possessions*. When these two words are compounded, they form the strange word *philarguros* — a term that depicts *an inordinate love of or an abnormal preoccupation with money or material possessions*.

People with this misdirected love are obsessed with having more and more. Obviously, if you have *philautos* — an unhealthy, inordinate self-love — in your life, you're going to sacrifice for yourself more than anyone else to get what you want. In fact, your altar will be *you*. You will sacrifice at the altar of *self*.

The Holy Spirit says at the very end of the age, people will be so self-infatuated, self-focused, and self-obsessed that they will inordinately spend money on themselves, to the neglect of helping others they should help. Thus, the ideas of *self-embellishment* and *greediness* are conveyed in the Greek word *philarguros* — the word translated as "covetous" in Second Timothy 3:2.

Taking into account the original Greek meaning, here is the *Renner Interpretive Version* (*RIV*) of the first part of Second Timothy 3:2:

> **Men will be self-focused, self-centered, self-absorbed, self-consumed, and in love with themselves more than anyone else. As a result of this self-love, they will be driven to obtain more and more and more....**

The result of making oneself top priority over all else produces a misdirected spending of money or excessive materialism. Although this is not meant in any way to condemn you, if you feel you have veered off track and have become selfish in your spending, take this opportunity to ask God for forgiveness and for the grace to put Him first and be more mindful to give to the needs of others.

Where We Put Our Money Reveals What We Really Love

Now, to be clear, it is God's will for you to be blessed and to prosper. However, He doesn't want you to become so self-focused that you never use your resources to advance the Gospel or help those in need. This is one reason He warns us, "…If riches increase, set not your heart upon them" (Psalm 62:10).

Jesus said, "For where your treasure is, there will your heart be also" (Matthew 6:21). If you want to know what is most important and most valuable to you, all you need to do is follow the money. Money talks — it tells the truth about what you cherish and what has captured the affection of your heart. If your bank statement shows that beyond your basic responsibilities, you spend most or all your money on yourself, your love is misdirected.

The Holy Spirit said society as a whole will be "covetous" (*philarguros*) in the last of the last days. Friend, we must listen to the Spirit's warning and guard ourselves from falling prey to this misdirected love for money and material possessions. First and foremost, we must decide to honor God by giving back to Him the tithe — a tenth of our income (*see* Malachi 3:10) — and dedicating our resources to Him, giving whatever He asks us to give. The care of widows and orphans and the support of missionaries who bring the Good News around the globe are all opportunities for us to bless others, store up eternal rewards, and keep ourselves from becoming covetous.

Who Is the 'Great Restrainer' in This Last-Days Scenario?

In Second Thessalonians 2, the apostle Paul talks about a force that is "withholding" the unveiling of the Antichrist — the one who's also called *the man of sin* and *the son of perdition*. This "restrainer" is also at work holding back the onslaught of evil that will enter and consume the earth at the end of the age. The Bible says:

> **And now ye know what withholdeth that he might be revealed in his time.**
>
> **For the mystery of iniquity doth already work: only he who now letteth will let, until he be taken out of the way.**

> And then shall that Wicked be revealed....
> — 2 Thessalonians 2:6-8

In these verses, the one that "withholdeth" and that "letteth" are one and the same. It is the Great Restrainer — the one holding back, postponing, and stalling the emergence of evil in the earth and the manifestation of the Antichrist after the rapture of Christ's Church.

A careful study of Scripture reveals that the Great Restrainer is *the Church*. This shows how powerful we are as long as we are here. Our very presence in the earth is restraining and holding back the coming of the Antichrist and even some of the manifestations of the Antichrist spirit that attempts to work full-force in the world today, such as an inordinate love of self and material possessions.

In the next lesson, we'll pick back up with Paul's discourse on the characteristics of a last-days society that as believers, we can observe as *signs of the times*.

STUDY QUESTIONS

> Study to shew thyself approved unto God, a workman that needeth not to be ashamed, rightly dividing the word of truth.
> — 2 Timothy 2:15

1. Take a few moments to reflect on the *Renner Interpretive Version* (*RIV*) of Second Timothy 3:1. How does this help you better understand the urgency of the times in which we live?
2. What does God say in Deuteronomy 8:17 and 18 about the purpose for wealth and how it comes to us? Is it possible to have a great deal of money and material possessions and not be happy? What does Ecclesiastes 5:19 say about the ability to enjoy what we've been given?
3. The Bible has much to say about money and earthly riches. Take time to look up these words of wisdom and jot down the recurring truths about wealth that God is communicating to you.
   - Psalm 39:6; 49:10
   - Ecclesiastes 2:18 (*AMP*)
   - Proverbs 23:5; 27:24
   - 1 Timothy 6:6-10; 17-19

- Matthew 6:19-21; 19:21
- Luke 12:33,34

PRACTICAL APPLICATION

> But be ye doers of the word, and not hearers only, deceiving your own selves.
> —James 1:22

1. As you read through this lesson, what part(s) especially hit you as being relevant and applicable to our present-day world? In what specific ways do you sense the Holy Spirit tugging at your heart?
2. Being *covetous* is having *an inordinate love of or an abnormal preoccupation with money or material possessions.* Be honest with yourself and God. Is this something you're dealing with? Take some time to look over your records of debits and credit-card statements. What do your spending habits reveal about who and what you love most? How might praying before making purchases help you break free from a covetous mindset?

LESSON 4

TOPIC

Snooty Agenda-Setters

SCRIPTURES

2 Timothy 3:1,2 — This know also, that in the last days perilous times shall come. For men shall be lovers of their own selves, covetous, boasters, proud....

GREEK WORDS

1. "lovers of their own selves" — φίλαυτος (*philautos*): from φίλος (*philos*) and αὐτός (*autos*); the word φίλος (*philos*) means to love or to be fond of, and it denotes the love, fondness, attraction, or romantic feelings one has for another; the word αὐτός (*autos*) means oneself; when compounded, it means love of self and actually describes inordinate

self-love, self-preoccupation, or one in love with and consumed with himself; self-absorbed; self-focused; inordinate self-love

2. "coveteous" — φιλάργυρος (*philarguros*): from φίλος (*philos*) and ἄργυρος (*arguros*); the word φίλος (*philos*) refers to love, fondness, attraction, and romance; the word ἄργυρος (*arguros*) is the word for silver or money; when compounded, it depicts an inordinate love of or an abnormal preoccupation with money or material possessions

3. "boasters" — ἀλαζών (*alazon*): one so committed to his own self-promotion and personal agenda that he is willing to exaggerate, overstate the facts, stretch the truth, embellish a story, and even lie if it will have a positive effect on his position or situation

4. "proud" — ὑπερήφανος (*huperephanos*): from ὑπερ (*huper*) and φανος (*phanos*); the word ὑπερ (*huper*) depicts something that is above or superior; the word φανος (*phanos*) means to be manifested; when compounded, it paints a picture of a person who sees himself above the rest of the crowd; one who is arrogant, haughty, high-and-mighty, impudent, and insolent; one who thinks he is intellectually advantaged above others

SYNOPSIS

In our first three lessons, we examined the Holy Spirit's warning through Paul in Second Timothy 3:1, which says, "This know also, that in the last days perilous times shall come." Here, the Spirit is telling us what is going to take place at the end of the age.

When we insert the original Greek meaning of the words in this verse, we see the *Renner Interpretive Version* (*RIV*) of Second Timothy 3:1 states:

> **You emphatically and categorically need to know with unquestionable certainty that in the very end of days — when time has sailed to its last port and no more time remains for the journey — that last season will stand in the midst of uncontrollable, unpredictable, hurtful, treacherous, and menacing times that will be emotionally difficult for people to bear.**

In the verses that follow, Paul begins to prophetically describe 25 characteristics of society at the very end of time — the chief one being an unhealthy, inordinate self-love. Out of this deeply flawed foundation, all other deviancies develop.

The emphasis of this lesson:

In addition to warning us against having an inordinate love of self and becoming covetous, the Holy Spirit also warns us that society in the last days will become saturated with those who are boasters and proud.

A Quick Overview of Second Timothy 3:2 From the Greek

In Second Timothy 3:2, the Bible says, "For men shall be lovers of their own selves, covetous, boasters, proud…." In the original Greek, this portion of the verse says:

> *"Esontai gar hoi anthropoi philautoi, philarguroi, alazonis, huperephanoi…."*

Here is a quick glance at the essential meaning of each of these Greek words:

- *esontai* – translated as "shall be"; this word is derived from the Greek word *eimi*, which literally means *"I am."* The use of this word tells us that when we come to the very end of the age and there are no other stopping-off points in time, society will be a self-focused, "I am" generation.

- *gar* – translated as "for"; this conjunction connects what is being said to the previous verse and helps us see what perilous things we can expect in the last days.

- *hoi anthropoi* – translated as "men"; this word is derived from the word *anthropos*, which describes *mankind at large*. The tense is plural, indicating that something will be a widespread epidemic in society.

- *philautoi* – translated as "lovers of their own selves"; this word is taken from the words *phileo* and *autos* and describes *self-love*.

- *philarguroi* – translated as "covetous"; this word is derived from the words *phileo* and *arguros* and essentially describes *an inordinate love of or an abnormal preoccupation with money or material possessions*.

- *alazonis* – translated as "boasters"; this is the plural form of *alazon*, and it depicts *one so committed to his own self-promotion he's willing to do or say anything to achieve his self-centered goals*.

- ***huperephanoi*** – translated as "proud"; this is a compound of the words *huper* and *phenoi*, and it essentially denotes *one who sees himself above everyone else.*

It is important to note that each word that ends in *oi* is *plural*, which indicates that these negative characteristics are not confined to a single person but to the masses of mankind. To understand what we can expect to see, let's take a closer look at the first four markings of the last-days society.

Society Will Be Steeped in *Love of Self*

Paul prophesied that the foremost evidence of the last-days society is that "men shall be lovers of their own selves" (*see* 2 Timothy 3:2). The phrase "lovers of their own selves" is the Greek word *philautoi*, which is from the words *phileo* and *autos*. The word *phileo* means *to have a fondness or an attraction for someone.* It is from the word *philos*, meaning *to love* or *to be fond of*, and it denotes *the love, fondness, attraction, or romantic feelings one has for another.*

The word *autos* is the Greek term for *oneself.* When compounded with *phileo* to form the new word *philautos*, it means *love of self* and actually describes *inordinate self-love, self-preoccupation,* or *one in love with and consumed with himself.* This word depicts one who is *self-absorbed* or *self-focused.*

The message the Holy Spirit is giving us is clear: In the last of the last days, society will be consumed with *love of self.* Since this is the case, it means people will be *philautos*, which means their focus and love will primarily be directed toward themselves. This means society will become *narcissistic, self-consumed, off-balance,* and *faulty at the core.*

Again, the word *philautoi* and its English translation are plural, indicating that this condition will be rampant throughout society. At the core, mankind in general will build their lives on a flawed foundation of self-love, causing society to become further and further lopsided and off-balance.

This is what the Holy Spirit prophesied through Paul regarding the condition of humanity at the end of the age. Consequently, society will have a "leaning syndrome," eventually resulting in selfishness on an epic scale, which leads us to the next point on the prophetic list given by the Spirit of God.

Self-Obsession Will Give Way to 'Covetousness'

The second end-time condition in society Paul noted is that people will be "covetous" (*see* 2 Timothy 3:2). This word is a compound of the words *phileo* and *arguros*. Again, *phileo* means *to have a fondness or an attraction for someone*. It is from the word *philos*, meaning *to love* or *to be fond of*, and it denotes *the love, fondness, attraction, or romantic feelings one has for another*. Usually, one would use this word to describe his or her feelings for another, not himself or herself.

The second part of the word "coveteous" in Greek is *arguros*, which is the word for *silver* or *money* and can also refer to *material possessions*. When *phileo* and *arguros* are compounded to form *philarguroi* (the plural form of *philarguros*), it depicts *an inordinate love of or an abnormal preoccupation with money or material possessions*.

Without question, the combining of *phileo* and *arguros* to form *philarguros* is very odd. It is made up of two words that would not usually be used together. In ancient times, this word was used to describe people who had excess money but refused to use it to help others because they were so fixated on doing what they wanted to satisfy their own needs. Hence, the age-old ideas of *self-embellishment* and *greediness* are embodied in the Greek word *philarguros*.

Here, the Holy Spirit is warning us that at the very end of the age, because people are *philautoi* — in love with themselves — they will develop an insatiable desire to have more and more wealth and material possessions. As a result of being self-obsessed, it will be difficult for them to say no to themselves, and therefore, they're going to make all their sacrifices at the altar of self.

This is one of the end-time conditions the Holy Spirit prophesied will take place in society at the end of the age. Keep in mind, as each of these vices is introduced, they will build one on top of the other — the foundation being an inordinate love of self (*philautos*). When society is built on self-love and self-fixation, everything else goes awry and continues to tilt in the wrong direction. That's why the Holy Spirit is telling us this. He wants us to make sure that we're not faulty at our own core or foundation.

'Boasters' Will Abound

The next deviation we can expect to see in society in the last of the last days is the rise of "boasters" (*see* 2 Timothy 3:2). This is the Greek word *alazonis*, which is the plural form of *alazon*, and it describes *one so committed to his own self-promotion and personal agenda that he is willing to exaggerate, overstate the facts, stretch the truth, embellish a story, and even lie if it will have a positive effect on his position or situation.*

In today's vernacular, we would liken the word *alazonis* to *situational ethics* — that is, the hurling away of fixed ethics or moral absolutes to embrace a "floating ethics" mode that is easily adapted to whatever one deems necessary at the moment. A good example of this would be politicians who change their ethics and policies to fit whatever the public wants to hear. They don't really say what they believe; they just say — and promise — what they believe best fits the desires of the crowd. A person with this mindset will do or say almost anything he feels is necessary to further a personal agenda, even if it clashes with his conscience, conviction, or the truth.

Unfortunately, today this twisted philosophy is being pushed in media, education, and in nearly every sphere of society. Evidence abounds revealing how far this delusion and a widespread mutiny against God and His Word have already advanced in the world today. We are witnesses of a society that has gone morally adrift and is regretfully being led astray by "boasters," as the Bible describes.

These leaders hold views that continually float, fluctuate, and shift. Their beliefs are affected by the ever-changing current of thought and by the most recently accepted norms, whatever they may be.

This way of thinking is perpetuated in the education of children and young people in schools and universities. Additionally, through the media and every other avenue possible, this worldview is being aggressively pushed by those who believe they have the right to subject everyone else — including Christians — to their own twisted moral code.

Believers who stick with the Word of God and refuse to go the way of the world have already been awakened to the reality that they're on a collision course with a culture in decline. This constant changing of moral standards and easy modification of what people believe or stand for could be included in this word "boasters" — the Greek word *alazonis*. All the "situational ethics" meanings we have discussed, including the flip-flopping on issues of morality, drastically altering one's belief system, and vacillating on issues of right and wrong are all signs of "boasters" in the very last days of this age.

The 'Proud' Will Push for Their Agenda

Closely connected with the exponential increase of boasters is an unprecedented rise in those the Bible calls "proud" (*see* 2 Timothy 3:2). This word "proud" is a translation of the Greek word *huperephanoi*, which is a compound of the words *huper* and *phanos*. The word *huper* depicts *something that is above* or *superior*, and the word *phanos* means *to be manifested*. When compounded, the new word *huperephanoi* paints a picture of a person who sees himself above the rest of the crowd. It is *one who is arrogant, haughty, high-and-mighty, impudent, and insolent.*

Those who are "proud" think they are intellectually advantaged above others. They are agenda-setters who believe they have the right to tell everyone else what to believe and what to do. These individuals are most clearly visible in the media, the political world, and the courts, in which they "snootily" promote themselves as the vanguards of society. These leaders see themselves as a more sophisticated group of people than everyone else, touting themselves as the rightful agenda-setters for society, culture, and the world.

Taking into account the original Greek meaning, here is the *Renner Interpretive Version* (*RIV*) of what we've discussed in Second Timothy 3:2 so far:

> **Men will be self-focused, self-centered, self-absorbed, self-consumed, and in love with themselves more than anyone else. And as a result of this self-love, they will be driven to obtain more and more and more. These boasters are so committed to their own agenda that they are willing to exaggerate, overstate the facts, stretch the truth, embellish a story, and even lie if it will get them the position, advantage, or goal they desire. They are arrogant, haughty, impudent, snooty, and insolent....**

Isn't it amazing how relevant the Bible is! What the Holy Spirit prophesied through Paul nearly 2,000 years ago is happening right before our eyes! With all these confirmed signs taking place, we know that Christ's return to rapture the Church is very near! And the revealing of the Antichrist will take place just after that.

Is the Antichrist Alive Right Now?

This question is being asked by many in this hour. With all the signs we are seeing taking place simultaneously, there is a high chance the Antichrist is living somewhere on the earth right now. No doubt, we're living at the very end of the age, and the Church — whom the Bible calls the Great Restrainer — is presently holding back evil and putting the brakes on the manifestation of the Antichrist. In fact, the apostle Paul tells us in **Second Thessalonians 2:7**:

> **For the mystery of iniquity doth already work: only he who now letteth will let, until he be taken out of the way.**

In this verse, the "he who now letteth" is the same "he" that will be taken out of the way, and as we saw in our previous lesson, this restraining force is the Church. The event being referred to when the Church is taken out of the way is what we know to be the Rapture.

Second Thessalonians 2:8 goes on to say:

> **And then shall that Wicked be revealed, whom the Lord shall consume with the spirit of his mouth, and shall destroy with the brightness of his coming.**

What we find within the context of these two verses is that the moment the Church is evacuated, the curtains will be pulled apart, and the Antichrist — that Wicked One — will be revealed, and he will step onto center stage.

Until the Church is gone, his identity will not be known.

STUDY QUESTIONS

> *Study to shew thyself approved unto God, a workman that needeth not to be ashamed, rightly dividing the word of truth.*
> — 2 Timothy 2:15

1. *Pride* is a major characteristic of a last-days society. What does the Bible say about this highly infectious menace in Proverbs 11:2; 16:18,19; 21:4; 29:23 and Psalm 119:21?
2. *Humility* is the only antidote for pride, and Jesus is the embodiment and giver of this exceedingly valuable virtue. According to

Matthew 11:28-30, how can you ensure humility is cultivated in your character? (Also consider Hebrews 12:2-4; John 13:1-17.)

3. Do you ever find yourself taking on the role of a *"boaster"—exaggerating, overstating the facts,* or *stretching the truth* in order to sway others to your position? Look at what Jesus says in Matthew 5:34-37 and what James says in James 4:13-16. How do these passages help you avoid the tendency?

PRACTICAL APPLICATION

> But be ye doers of the word, and not hearers only, deceiving your own selves.
> —James 1:22

1. One of the primary meanings of the word "boasters" in Greek is people who hold to *situational ethics*. Rather than maintain moral absolutes, they embrace a "floating ethics" mode that is easily adapted to whatever they deem necessary at the moment? Have you ever been the victim of someone practicing such ethics? Take a moment and briefly share what happened. How did God help you handle the situation?

2. According to the original Greek meaning, those who are "proud" are *arrogant, haughty, impudent, snooty,* and *insolent.* They are agenda-setters who believe they have the right to tell everyone else what to believe and what to do. Who in society would you say falls into this category and what are they trying to force on society (and on you)? Pray and ask the Holy Spirit to show you what you can do to push back against their evil agenda.

3. The Holy Spirit said that those living at the end of the age would feel like they were *standing in the very middle of perilous times.* What specific manifestations of chaos and confusion seem to be "surrounding you on all sides"? Pray and ask the Holy Spirit to show you what you should do in response to these external realities He predicted would occur.

LESSON 5

TOPIC
An Evil Last-Days Agenda

SCRIPTURES
2 Timothy 3:2 — For men shall be lovers of their own selves, covetous, boasters, proud, blasphemers, disobedient to parents....

GREEK WORDS
1. "boasters" — ἀλαζών (*alazon*): one so committed to his own self-promotion and personal agenda that he is willing to exaggerate, overstate the facts, stretch the truth, embellish a story, and even lie if it will have a positive effect on his position or situation
2. "proud" — ὑπερήφανος (*huperephanos*): from ὑπερ (*huper*) and φανος (*phanos*); the word ὑπερ (*huper*) depicts something that is above or superior; the word φανος (*phanos*) means to be manifested; when compounded, it paints a picture of a person who sees himself above the rest of the crowd; one who is arrogant, haughty, high-and-mighty, impudent, and insolent; one who thinks he is intellectually advantaged above others
3. "blasphemers" — βλασφημέω (*blasphemos*): to slander; to accuse; to speak against; to speak derogatory words for the purpose of injuring or harming one's reputation; signifies profane, foul, unclean language; can refer to blaspheming the divine, but in general, it is any derogatory speech intended to defame, injure, or harm another's reputation; the broader meaning includes any type of debasing, derogatory, nasty, shameful, ugly speech or behavior
4. "disobedient" — ἀπειθής (*apeithes*): from the πείθω (*peitho*), which means to persuade or to convince; but when it is transformed into ἀπειθής (*apeithes*), it means unpersuadable, uncontrollable, or unleadable; no longer able to persuade, control, lead, or exercise authority over; a loss of control; a lack of ability to persuade or lead

SYNOPSIS

Without question, misdirected love negatively affects everything in the life of an individual as well as in society as a whole. The Holy Spirit makes this clear through the apostle Paul in his second letter to his spiritual apprentice Timothy. This eye-opening prophecy, which was written nearly 2,000 ago, was not written to *scare* us, but to *prepare* us for navigating these last of the last days. If we'll take these words to heart, the Spirit of God will use them to help us examine our own lives and take the steps necessary to keep ourselves from falling prey to these ungodly attitudes and characteristics.

The emphasis of this lesson:

Two additional prophetic signs that will decidedly mark the end of the age are a severe increase in blasphemous behavior and children who are disobedient to parents. Both negative characteristics are abounding in society today.

A REVIEW OF THE FIRST FOUR CHARACTERISTICS OF SOCIETY IN THE LAST OF THE LAST DAYS

Writing under the inspiration of the Holy Spirit, Paul informed us, "…That in the last days perilous times shall come. For men shall be lovers of their own selves, covetous, boasters, proud, blasphemers, disobedient to parents…" (2 Timothy 3:1,2). Thus far, we have examined four distinct defects of the last-days society. To help us more fully grasp what the Holy Spirit is telling us, here is a quick recap of what we've studied:

'Men Shall Be Lovers of Their Own Selves'

The words "shall be" are a translation of the Greek word *esontai*, which is derived from the word *eimi* and literally means *"I am."* The use of this word tells us that when we come to the very end of the age, society as a whole will become a self-focused, narcissistic, "I am" generation.

Just go to the local bookstore and see how many *self-help* books there are. Although getting help for what we're struggling with is not wrong, the vast number of such books is evidence that we're living in an age where people are fixated on themselves. The Holy Spirit prophesied through Paul that a day was coming when self-obsession would rule, and that day is here in an epidemic fashion.

Next, notice the word "men," which is a translation of the Greek words *hoi anthropoi*. The word *anthropoi* is the plural form of *anthropos*, the word for *man*, but when it becomes *hoi anthropoi*, it describes *mankind at large*. Because the tense is plural, it indicates this issue will be widespread in society.

Specifically, mankind at large will become "lovers of their own selves." This is the Greek word *philautoi*, which is a combination of the words *phileo* and *autos* and basically describes *an inordinate, unhealthy love of self*. By using this word, the Holy Spirit is telling us that the end-time society will be *self-absorbed, self-focused, and narcissistic*. Out of this misdirection of love, all other dysfunctions flow.

'Covetous'

In this self-obsessed condition, society will become more and more "covetous" (*see* 2 Timothy 3:2). We've seen that this word is a translation of the Greek word *philarguroi* — from the words *phileo* and *arguros*. The word *phileo* means *to love* or *to have a fondness or attraction for someone*, and the word *arguros* is essentially the Greek word for *money* or *material possessions*. When compounded to form the word *philarguroi*, it depicts *an inordinate love of or an abnormal preoccupation with money or material possessions*. As a result of people being in love with themselves, they will use most of their resources on themselves, living embellished, pampered lives.

As we noted, this word was used in ancient Greek to describe people who had adequate resources and could help others but chose not to because they selfishly sought to spend everything on themselves. Being aware of this end-time tendency should make us want to look at our own spending and honestly ask ourselves, *What and who am I spending most of my money on? Am I giving to God what is His? And am I helping others in need?* If we're spending everything we have on ourselves, it might be that we've fallen victim to the spirit of the age. Do you see why you need to know what the Holy Spirit said about the end of the age?

'Boasters'

Along with an exponential increase of covetousness, the end of the age will also usher in a new breed of "boasters" (*see* 2 Timothy 3:2). As noted, this word "boasters" is a translation of the Greek word *alazonis*, which is the plural form of the word *alazon*. It describes *a braggart* or *one so committed to his own self-promotion and personal agenda that he is willing to exaggerate, overstate the facts, stretch the truth, embellish a story, and even lie if it will have a positive effect on his position or situation.*

Today, we would call this *situational ethics.* Those adhering to such a moral code will say or do anything and quickly change what they believe if it will get them what they want. Sadly, this deviant tendency has become commonplace — especially in the media and in the political world. For instance, politicians will often change their stories or stance from one day to the next — at times denying the very words they previously said. Even some of today's major corporations have flip-flopped on moral issues to adapt to an ever-changing culture of political correctness.

This hurling away of fixed ethics or moral absolutes is a major sign of the last of the last days. The "boasters" the Holy Spirit prophesied about will play a major role in how the devil will bring end-time lawlessness into the mainstream of society and ultimately install the Antichrist as the world leader.

'Proud'

Along with boasters, Paul said many in society will become "proud" (*see* 2 Timothy 3:2). This word "proud" is the Greek word *huperephanoi*, which is the plural form of *huperephanos*, a compound of the words *huper* and *phanos*. The word *huper* means *above* and depicts *something that is superior*; and the word *phanos* means *to be manifested.* When compounded to form the word *huperephanoi*, it depicts *a person who sees himself above the rest of the crowd.* It is *one who is arrogant, haughty, high-and-mighty, snooty, impudent, and insolent.* Those who are "proud" think they are *intellectually advantaged above others* and therefore possess the right to set the agenda for everyone else.

Today, we see the word "proud" clearly on display in the media, in the political world, and in the courts, in which many "snootily" promote themselves as the vanguards of society. These leaders see themselves as a more sophisticated set of people than everyone else, marketing themselves as the rightful agenda-setters for society, culture, and the world.

By using this word *huperephanoi* — translated here as "proud" — Paul is telling us that an anti-God, anti-Bible, end-time society will also display a "we-know-better-than-you" attitude toward those who adhere to biblical truth as their standard. Does that sound anything like the attitudes of people we're dealing with today?

These self-imposed agenda-setters view anyone who holds to time-tested morals and biblical values as a hindrance to the new world they're striving to create, and to a great degree, that is true! We who refuse to budge from our Bible-based way of living are a part of the restraining force Paul talks about in Second Thessalonians 2:6,7. As we maintain our godly convictions and shine the light of truth into a darkened world, we are literally holding back the onslaught of evil that will eventually be released and engulf society.

Society Will Be Filled With 'Blasphemers'

In addition to people being increasingly proud, we will also see an increased presence of those the Bible calls "blasphemers" (*see* 2 Timothy 3:2). This is the Greek word *blasphemoi*, which is the plural form of *blasphemos*, and it means *to slander, to accuse, to speak against, or to speak derogatory words for the purpose of injuring or harming one's reputation*. It signifies *profane, foul, unclean language* and can refer to *blaspheming the divine*, but in general, it is *any derogatory speech intended to defame, injure, or harm another's reputation*. The broader meaning of this word includes *any type of debasing, derogatory, nasty, shameful, or ugly speech or behavior intended to humiliate someone.*

Blasphemous language has become such a regular component of speech in our time that even taboo words — once considered vulgar and extremely offensive — have found their way into mainstream conversation. Historically, such language was considered impolite and rude, but we have devolved so terribly in our times that in order to avoid hearing profanity, we now have to install special devices to "bleep" it out of the programming.

This problem is not just limited to blasphemous language. The word *blasphemoi* also describes *blasphemous behaviors*. Rather than attempt to list all the actions in question, suffice it to say that behaviors and lifestyles that were once viewed as immoral are now being paraded on television, in social media, and in movies nearly every day. What God judged Sodom and Gomorrah for is now brazenly applauded and celebrated by eminent professors, celebrities, educators, media giants, corporations, and the courts. Actions the Bible calls "blasphemous" are being propagandized to a younger generation, desensitizing and conditioning them to accept the bizarre, the barbaric, and the perverse as normal.

Please don't misread this as being judgmental. We are to have compassion for anyone who is trapped in deception and offer them the message of freedom through Jesus. At the same time, we need to realize that the viral proliferation of blasphemy in all its forms is an assault against humanity — especially the impressionable minds of children.

It is also important to note that the word *blasphemos* denotes *speaking slanderously* or *railing against someone by bringing abusive, debasing, degrading accusations against those with whom one does not agree*. Although this includes the use of "curse words," it is predominantly *rude, crude speech*. In the context of Second Timothy 3:2, Paul was telling us that high-minded agenda-setters will speak slanderously and bring abusive, debasing, and degrading accusations against those with whom they disagree. Because they see themselves as *intellectually advantaged* above others whom they deem to be primitive or resistant to "progress and change," they will disdain, mock, slander, and speak ill of them.

Frankly, in the last days, it will seem as if manners have been removed altogether, and people will begin to speak things that formerly would have been considered shameful. The truth is, it is downright shocking what is said in movies, on television, and by our elected officials. The rude and crude things people say to and about each other — and the insulting jokes they make about God — perfectly fulfill this word "blasphemers."

Children Will Become 'Disobedient to Parents'

What else will grow out of an inordinate, unhealthy love of self? The Bible says children will become "disobedient to parents" (*see* 2 Timothy 3:2). The word "disobedient" here is the Greek word *apeithes*, a derivative of the word *peitho*, which means *to persuade or to convince*. However, when an "a" is placed on the front of it, transforming it into *apeithes*, it cancels or reverses the meaning. Hence, *apeithes* means *unpersuadable, uncontrollable*, or *unleadable*. One who is "disobedient" is one who is *no longer able to be persuaded, controlled, or led*; he or she is one who will not allow anyone to *exercise authority over* him or her. This word also depicts *a loss of control* or *a lack of ability to persuade or lead*.

By using this word *apeithes*, the Holy Spirit is prophesying that parenthood will come under assault, and parents will be pressured to surrender their authority to lead their own children. As they begin to feel the loss of ability to *persuade*, *control*, *lead*, or *exercise authority over* their children — which in large part is already occurring — children will no longer submit to or follow the leadership of their parents. They will deny their parents' right to lead them and will even assert their "rights" to make decisions for themselves without parental influence or intervention — including decisions that in many cases will be life-altering or detrimental to their long-term well-being.

Friend, this is happening right now. Every day, children are being told in school, "You are your own person in charge of your own life and destiny. You have your rights, and you shouldn't allow your parents to enforce rules or outdated religious beliefs on you that you don't agree with. You can make decisions for yourself, and you don't have to inform your parents about what you're doing."

Clearly, this prophecy from Second Timothy 3:2 — of children being "disobedient to parents" — is being fulfilled before our very eyes. It is one of the chief characteristics of the last-days generation when people — including children — are so self-obsessed and self-focused that they believe they are the center of their own world. It's during these dark days that many parents will find themselves attempting to *negotiate* with their kids rather than lead and discipline them as God expects them to do. And children will believe they have the right to make all the decisions for their life by themselves, without informing their parents or asking for their permission.

Who could have ever imagined we would arrive at such a place? Yet counselors, court advocates, and clergy will all confirm this radical trend to be true. In the midst of this last-days society — when situational ethics are ruling, moral absolutes have been thrown to the wind, and foul language and uncivil behavior are the norm — the Bible says there will also be an epidemic of disobedience to parents.

Putting the original Greek meanings of all these words together, here is the *Renner Interpretive Version* (*RIV*) for the first part of Second Timothy 3:2:

> **Men will be self-focused, self-centered, self-absorbed, self-consumed, and in love with themselves more than anyone else. As a result of this self-love, they will be driven to obtain more and more and more. These boasters are so committed to their own agenda that they are willing to exaggerate, overstate the facts, stretch the truth, embellish a story, and even lie if it**

will get them the position, advantage, or goal they desire. They are arrogant, haughty, impudent, snooty, and insolent. They disdain, mock, slander, and speak ill of anyone who stands in the way of their ideology, and they freely use foul language. In this climate, parents will no longer be able to persuade, control, lead, or exercise authority over their own children....

As dark and ominous as all this may sound, God doesn't want us to shrink back in fear. Instead, He wants us to arise and shine and let His glory pierce the darkness of the world around us (*see* Isaiah 60:1,2). As we seek His face and receive His grace daily, we can live above the evil that is overwhelming the world in these final hours, and we can give godly solutions to those who desperately need answers.

When Will the Mark of the Beast Be Given to People?

It's important to understand the 25 last-days signs that Paul prophesied about by the power of the Holy Spirit. But many are concerned about other end-time events that they feel might also affect them and those they love. For example, with all the high-tech developments, the surge of AI, and all the talk of a cashless society, many believers are asking when the mark of the beast will be given. To accurately answer this important question, we turn to Scripture, which says that the mark of the beast will be issued when the Antichrist is in power. But for him to be in power, he must first be revealed.

Second Thessalonians 2:7 and 8 says that before the Antichrist is revealed, the Church will be raptured. Looking at these verses, it says, "For the mystery of iniquity doth already work: only he who now letteth will let, until he be taken out of the way. And *then* shall that Wicked be revealed...."

As we noted, "he that now letteth" and the "he" that will be "taken out of the way" are one and the same — the Great Restrainer — that is, the Church. So once the Church is suddenly removed, THEN "...that Wicked [will] be revealed..." (2 Thessalonians 2:8).

"That Wicked" is the Antichrist, and his identity won't be made known to the world until the Church is raptured. In that synchronized moment, the Church will go up and the curtain will come down to reveal the identity of the Antichrist. But all of that is going to occur *after* the rapture of the Church, which means the mark of the beast won't be given until after the Church has been evacuated.

STUDY QUESTIONS

> **Study to shew thyself approved unto God, a workman that needeth not to be ashamed, rightly dividing the word of truth.**
> — 2 Timothy 2:15

1. As a parent, grandparent, or guardian who has been entrusted with the privilege of raising children, it is good to reflect on what God desires and expects of us. Look up these passages of Scripture and identify God's instruction in each regarding the rearing of your children.
   - Proverbs 22:6; Ephesians 6:4; Colossians 3:21
   - Deuteronomy 6:4-9
   - Psalm 78:1-8
   - Proverbs 13:24; 19:18; 22:15; 23:13

2. How are you doing in these endeavors? In which areas do you need God's grace to help you come up higher?

3. Be honest. Have you become so desensitized to blasphemous language and behaviors in the world that you now consider it normal? Are you spiritually calloused to what you're seeing and hearing? What is the number-one thing you can pray and ask the Holy Spirit to give you to soften and change your heart? (*See* Deuteronomy 10:12; Joshua 24:14; Ecclesiastes 12:13; Psalm 34:9-13; Isaiah 11:2,3.)

PRACTICAL APPLICATION

> **But be ye doers of the word, and not hearers only, deceiving your own selves.**
> — James 1:22

1. In what particular ways are you personally witnessing the disintegration of honor and respect for parents? How about for authority in general? (Consider what is being offered through movies and the mainstream media, as well as real-life examples.)

2. Can you think of any areas in your life where you have allowed the influence of the world to pollute your view? Is there a particular biblical standard you once held tightly to, but in recent years, you have lowered your standard to accommodate people — even family members who are living outside of God's will and His ways? What are

these areas where you have compromised your convictions and beliefs and adapted to your environment?
3. What do you sense the Spirit of God prompting you to do to realign yourself to the unchanging truth of His Word?

LESSON 6

TOPIC
A World Full of Ingrates

SCRIPTURES
2 Timothy 3:1,2 — *This know also, that in the last days perilous times shall come. For men shall be lovers of their own selves, covetous, boasters, proud, blasphemers, disobedient to parents, unthankful, unholy.*

GREEK WORDS
1. "disobedient" — ἀπειθής (*apeithes*): from πείθω (*peitho*), which means to persuade or to convince; but when it is transformed into ἀπειθής (*apeithes*), it means unpersuadable, uncontrollable, or unleadable; no longer able to persuade, control, lead, or exercise authority over; a loss of control; a lack of ability to persuade or lead
2. "unthankful" — ἀχάριστος (*acharistos*): from χάριστος (*charistos*), which means thankful; when an ἀ (a) is attached to the front of the word, it reverses the condition, changing the meaning to unthankful or ungrateful; it pictures a person or group of people who were once thankful but who have become unappreciative and unthankful; entitled

SYNOPSIS
Few things affect our overall well-being more than an attitude of ingratitude. *Unthankfulness* or ingratitude, is another prevalent mindset at the end of the age that we must guard against. Although society will become *infused* by this gangrenous way of thinking, we can choose to maintain a thankful heart — despite what is going on around us. If we develop

the habit of purposely counting our blessings, we will experience the far-reaching, positive effects that a thankful heart brings.

The emphasis of this lesson:

An unthankful attitude portrays a person who is ungrateful for what others have done for him and unappreciative of what one has. This attitude will permeate through society at the end of the age and will manifest as a sense of entitlement in which many people think "everyone owes me."

A REVIEW OF OUR ANCHOR VERSE

Writing under the anointing of the Holy Spirit nearly 2,000 years ago, the apostle Paul urgently voiced these words in his second letter to Timothy:

> **This know also, that in the last days perilous times shall come.**
> **— 2 Timothy 3:1**

As we've noted, every word in the New Testament has value and is placed in the Bible for a reason, and this verse is a perfect example. Here's a quick review of the original Greek meaning of the words in this passage along with their English translations.

"This Know Also" — In Greek, this is written *touto de ginōske*, which is a stronger, more emphatic statement. The word *touto* means *this* or *explicitly this*, and the little word *de* is a conjunction, which here is used like an exclamation mark. We could translate these two words to say, *"This emphatically."*

Then Paul inserted the word *ginōske*, which is the direct form of the word *ginōsko*, meaning *to know*. Thus, these three words together could be translated, *"This categorically and unmistakably know."* These words are the equivalent of the Holy Spirit raising His voice and reaching out through the passages of Scripture to grab hold of us and shake us to attention. It's as if He is urgently saying, *This is something that must be known; it must be understood, and it must be embraced.* As we've noted, Paul was about to reveal incredible events that would occur at the end of the age — not so that we'd be afraid, but that we'd be aware of what's coming so we can avoid the pitfalls.

"That" — This is the next word Paul added. It is the Greek word *hoti*, which would best be described as *a pointer word* because it points to the major emphasis of what the Holy Spirit is communicating. Specifically, He is pointing to the undeniable fact that "...In the last days perilous times shall come" (2 Timothy 3:1).

"In the Last Days" — The word "in" is the little Greek word *en*, and it means *to be inside something*. Literally, Paul was saying that inside the sphere of the last days, something would take place.

In Greek, the words for "last days" are *eschatais hēmerais*, and as we've seen, the word *eschastais* was a word used to describe *something that is absolutely final*; it is *the ultimate end of a thing*. For example, you could use this word *eschatais* to describe the last day of a week, but only the *last* day. Likewise, it could describe the last month of the year, but only the *last* month.

Moreover, the word *eschastais* was used by the Greeks in a geographical sense to describe *the point that was furthest away*, and in a navigational context, it described *the last port of call for a ship*. Although the ship had many stopping points along the way, when it finally arrived at this port, it was the very last stop. No one could go any further once they arrived at the *eschastais* — it was the ultimate end of the journey.

Paul's use of this word tells us he was not talking about the entire 2,000-year, last-days period. Instead, he was talking about the timeframe we would call the very last days — when humanity has sailed to its last port and no more time remains for the journey. It is at that point that *perilous times shall come*.

"Perilous Times Shall Come" — Interestingly, in Greek, the word order here is *shall come perilous times*. The phrase "shall come" is a translation of the word *enstesontai*, which is a compound of the words *en*, meaning *to be inside something*, and the word *histémi*, meaning *to stand*. When these words are joined to form the word *enstesontai*, it pictures *one that is standing in the middle of something*. In fact, this person is surrounded by something on every side; it's standing all around him. We could say he's encumbered by it everywhere he looks. Whatever the Holy Spirit is describing is something that will burden society at the end of the age, making people feel stuck in the middle of something inescapable.

Specifically, society will be surrounded on all sides by "perilous times." We've seen that this phrase is a translation of the Greek words *kairoi chalepoi*. The word *kairoi* is the plural form of the word *kairós* — the term for *seasons*, *times*, or *opportunities*. The fact that this word is plural here indicates that when we've sailed to the very end of the age and no more time is left for the journey, we'll know it, because we're going to come face to face with "perilous" seasons, times, and opportunities. The word "perilous" here is *chalepoi*, which is the plural form of *chalepos*, and it describes *menacing, difficult, treacherous times*. Without question, these are the days we are living in.

Signs the Spirit Said We Would See at the End of the Age

In **Second Timothy 3:2**, we are warned by eight specific words and phrases that will simultaneously characterize the last of the last days. Paul wrote:

> **For men shall be lovers of their own selves, covetous, boasters, proud, blasphemers, disobedient to parents, unthankful, unholy.**

Like verse 1, this second verse of chapter 3 is jampacked with meaning. Here's a quick review of the original Greek meaning of these words and phrases along with their English translations.

"[There] Shall Be" — This phrase is a translation of the Greek word *esontai*, and it is from the word *eimi*, which means *I am*. By using this word, the Holy Spirit is telling us that at the end of the age, the world will be so self-centered and self-focused, it will become the *I am* generation, living for itself above all else.

"Men" — In Greek, the next two words are *hoi anthrōpoi*. The word *anthrōpoi* is the plural form of *anthropos*, which is the term for *man*, but when it is coupled with *hoi* and becomes *hoi anthrōpoi*, it means *all mankind*. This indicates that what is going to happen will spread to all humanity. At the very end of the age, a widespread problem is going to infect the world: Mankind will be *lovers of themselves*.

"Lovers of Their Own Selves" — This phrase is a translation of the Greek word *philautoi*, which is the plural form of *philautos*. It is a compound of the words *philos* and *autos*. The word *philos* means *to love* or *to be fond of*, and it denotes *the love, fondness, attraction, or romantic feelings one has for another*. And the word *autos* describes *oneself*. When compounded, they form the word *philautos*, meaning *love of self* and it describes *inordinate* *self-love, self-preoccupation,* or *one in love with and consumed with himself.* It presents the idea of one who is *self-focused, self-centered,* and *self-absorbed.*

This is the picture of a person who is fixated on himself, infatuated with himself, and loves himself more than he loves his spouse, his family, his country, or anything else. In his eyes, he's the top priority in his life, and he's so in love with himself that it paves the way for the next problem — being *covetous.*

"Covetous" — This is the very strange word *philargyroi,* which is from the words *phileo* and *arguros.* Again, *phileo* means *to have a fondness or an attraction for someone,* and it is from the word *philos,* meaning *to love* or *to be fond of.* It most often denotes *the love, fondness, attraction, or romantic feelings one has for another.*

The second part of the word for "coveteous" is *arguros,* which is the word for *silver* or *money* and can also refer to *material possessions.* When *phileo* and *arguros* are compounded to form *philargyroi* (the plural form of *philarguros*), it depicts *an inordinate love of or an abnormal preoccupation with money or material possessions.*

When a person is enamored with himself and is the center of his world (*philautos*), it's easy to see how he would develop a preoccupation with money and material possessions and begin spending most of what he had on himself. In ancient times, this word was used to describe people who had excess money, but refused to use it to help others because they were so fixated on satisfying their own needs. Hence, the age-old ideas of *self-embellishment* and *greediness* are embodied in the Greek word *philarguros.* This inability to say no to oneself depicts consumerism on a scale that is out of control.

"Boasters" — The third crippling characteristic of society at the very end of the age is the increase in what the Bible calls "boasters" — the Greek word *alazones.* Basically, this word describes what we would call *situational ethics* — when people flip-flop on morals, changing their positions to preserve their best interest and get ahead. They're willing to say or do anything — even lie — if it will get them the position or advantage they desire.

"Proud" — Closely connected with *boasters* is a fourth category of dysfunctional people the Scripture calls "proud." This is the Greek word *huperephanoi,* which is a compound of the words *huper* and *phanoi.* The word *huper* means *above* and depicts *a position of superiority,* and the word *phanoi*, which is plural, is a form of the word *phanos* and means *to be manifested*. When these words are joined together to form *huperephanoi* — translated here as "proud" — it describes *a person who sees himself above the rest of the crowd*. It is *one who is arrogant, haughty, high-and-mighty, snooty, impudent, and insolent*.

Those who are "proud" think they're *intellectually advantaged above others* and therefore possess the right to set the agenda for everyone else. The fact that the Holy Spirit prompted Paul to use this word tells us that at the end of the age, wicked men will declare themselves to be the agenda-setters and vanguards for society. They will dictate to everyone else what they're to believe and do and they will attempt to create a new world order. This is precisely what this word *huperephanoi* means.

"Blasphemers" — Along with the proud, we find the next display of evil that will abound in the last of the last days, which are "blasphemers." In Greek, this is the word *blasphemoi*, which is the plural form of the word *blasphemos*, and it means *to slander, to accuse, to speak against*, or *to speak derogatory words for the purpose of injuring or harming one's reputation*. It signifies *profane, foul, unclean language* and can refer to *blaspheming the divine*, but in general, it is *any derogatory speech intended to defame, injure, or harm another's reputation*.

Certainly, you would agree that we're living in a day when vulgar language is everywhere. From television and movies to social media and music, who would ever have imagined we would hear the kind of things that freely flow unashamedly from the lips of so many? Our society is saturated with debasing, derogatory, nasty, shameful, and ugly speech — all intended to humiliate others.

Interestingly, the word *blasphemo* also describes vulgar *behavior* that goes against the Word of God. What is offered as "entertainment" on television and at the box office is downright shocking. The rude and crude things people say about and do to each other — and the insulting jokes they make about God — perfectly demonstrate this word "blasphemers."

"Disobedient to Parents" — This phrase is a translation of the Greek words *goneusin apeithes*. The word *goneusin* means *to parents*, and the word *apeithes* is a form of the Greek word *peíthō*, which means *to persuade* or *to convince*. However, when the letter "a" is added to the front and it becomes *apeithes*, the original meaning is negated, and it means *unpersuadable*, *uncontrollable*, or *unleadable*. In this condition, parents are *no longer able to persuade, control, lead*, or *exercise authority over* their children.

In a last-days society where situational ethics reign, fixed moral absolutes are thrown to the wind, and foul language and blasphemous behaviors become commonplace, there will also emerge an epidemic of children who are "disobedient to parents." Again, this word depicts *a complete loss of control* or *a lack of ability to persuade, to lead*, or *to influence*.

By using the phrase *disobedient to parents*, the Holy Spirit is prophetically forecasting an unusual period at the end of the last days when parenthood will come under assault as parents begin to feel the loss of their ability to lead their own children. Rather than directing and guiding them, parents will find themselves trying to *negotiate* with their kids.

Friends, this is happening right now, and what makes matters worse is what many children are being told and taught in school. School officials say, "You don't have to do what your parents say or believe what they believe. You're in charge of your own life and your own destiny, and you shouldn't allow your parents to enforce rules or doctrines of faith that you don't agree with."

This is what the Holy Spirit prophesied would take place at the very end of the last days. Children will be disobedient (*apeithes*) to parents.

An Epidemic of Entitlement Will Also Grip Society

Paul continued to expound on his prophetic insights regarding what will transpire in society at the end of the age, saying, "For men shall be lovers of their own selves, covetous, boasters, proud, blasphemers, disobedient to parents, *unthankful*..." (2 Timothy 3:2). This word "unthankful" is the Greek word *acharistoi*, a form of the word *charistoi*, which is from the word *charis*, the word for *grace*.

The word *charistoi* is the plural form of *charistos*, which describes *one who has a thankful attitude, a grateful attitude*, or *an appreciative attitude*. However, when you put an "a" on the front of it, the original meaning is cancelled or reversed. Hence, the word *acharistos* describes *a person, people, and even nations that once were very grateful to God for everything they had, but they lost their sense of gratitude*. They're *no longer thankful* and *no longer appreciative*. In fact, those who have an attitude of entitlement aren't thankful for anything at all because they believe they deserve everything.

By using this word *acharistoi* — translated here as "unthankful"— the Holy Spirit is prophesying that at the end of the age, society will become filled with *ingrates*. Those who were once thankful for and appreciative of all they have will become *unthankful, ungrateful*, and *unappreciative*. An epidemic of entitlement will spread throughout the world, and the masses will adopt an "everybody owes me" attitude.

Unthankfulness is so detrimental to people's lives that Jesus connects it with evil in Luke 6:35. Indeed, in God's eyes, it is spiritually criminal not to be thankful for what we have in life — even if it seems like we have little compared to other people's blessings. Any person (or nation or a society) that has become unthankful is headed down a destructive path that will eventually lead him into a state of unholiness. This will be our focus in our next lesson.

Questions and Answers With Rick Renner

In the program, Rick answered the following question from one of our viewers.

Q. What happens to us when we die?

A. The question of an afterlife is on the minds of many. For believers, the answer is very clear: To be absent from the body is to be present with the Lord (*see* 2 Corinthians 5:8). Writing under the unction of the Holy Spirit, the apostle Paul said that when we die, our spirit is absent from our physical body but is present with the Lord. That means the split second we breathe our last physical breath, our spirit departs to be with Jesus!

In the meantime, our body will lie in the grave waiting for the great resurrection. On the day when Jesus comes to rapture the Church, the bodies of all the saints who have gone on to be with Him in Heaven are going to be resurrected. In that moment, their bodies will be raised back to life — totally new and incorruptible — and they'll be rejoined with their spirits. What an amazing day that will be! And it's coming sooner than we think!

STUDY QUESTIONS

> Study to shew thyself approved unto God, a workman that needeth not to be ashamed, rightly dividing the word of truth.
> — 2 Timothy 2:15

1. Taking your words and actions into account, would your heavenly Father consider you a *thankful* and *grateful* person or one that is *unthankful* and *ungrateful*?
2. The prerequisite to happiness is being *thankful*. No one can truly be happy with an ungrateful attitude. According to First Thessalonians 5:18 and Psalm 100:4, how important is *thankfulness* in God's eyes — and ears? (Also consider Colossians 1:12-14; 3:15.)
3. Carefully consider the words of King David in Psalm 103:1-5 and Paul's words in First Corinthians 15:57; Second Corinthians 2:14 and 9:15. How do these passages move your heart?

PRACTICAL APPLICATION

> But be ye doers of the word, and not hearers only,
> deceiving your own selves.
> —James 1:22

1. Take a few moments to be honest with yourself and God, asking and answering these questions:

    - *Do I show genuine gratitude for what God has done for me? If so, how?*

    - *Do I express genuine appreciation to others who have been a blessing to my life? If so, how?*

    - *Do I — or my children/grandchildren — have an attitude of entitlement, or do I (we) understand that hard work is required to be rewarded?*

2. Being thankful is often a *choice*, and it begins with *purposely remembering* the countless blessings God has provided. When was the last time you sat down and made a list of the things you are truly thankful for that God has done in your life? Take time now to reflect on and write down all He has done for you, including all the times He miraculously protected you and showed you mercy.

LESSON 7

TOPIC
The Dark Connection Between Unthankfulness and Unholiness

SCRIPTURES
2 Timothy 3:1,2 — This know also, that in the last days perilous times shall come. For men shall be lovers of their own selves, covetous, boasters, proud, blasphemers, disobedient to parents, **unthankful, unholy**.

GREEK WORDS
1. "unthankful" — ἀχάριστος (*acharistos*): from χάριστος (*charistos*), which means thankful; when an ἀ (*a*) is attached to the front of the word, it reverses the condition, changing the meaning to unthankful or ungrateful; it pictures a person or group of people who were once thankful but who have become unappreciative and unthankful; entitled
2. "unholy" — ἀνόσιος (*anosios*): from ὅσιος (*hosios*), which depicts a person or group of people that are reverent, respectful, and God-fearing; but when an ἀ (*a*) is attached to it, it has a canceling effect, therefore, it means that what was once holy has become unholy; what was once reverent has become irreverent; what was once God-fearing has lost its fear of God; can be translated irreverent and disrespectful; depicts those who have lost a fear of God and whose way of thinking and outward actions have become ill-mannered, impure, unclean, lewd, indecent, crude, coarse, vulgar, offensive, and rude

SYNOPSIS
In our last lesson, we learned that another major indicator we have reached the end of the age is a prevalent attitude of *unthankfulness*. You don't have to look long or hard to find this element pervading every area of our Western culture. The Holy Spirit let us know in advance that this was coming, worldwide, so we could prepare for it and not be swallowed up by an entitlement mindset. This prophetic insight demonstrates just

how much He loves us and wants to equip us not only to survive, but to *thrive* in this hour.

The emphasis of this lesson:

When people cease to be thankful and lose their reverential fear of God, a process begins in which they spiritually backslide and eventually become unholy. Left unchecked, they become more and more irreverent, disrespectful, and void of the fear of God.

The *Renner Interpretive Version* (*RIV*) of Second Timothy 3:1

Paul's message in Second Timothy was not only to his young apprentice, but also to believers throughout all generations. Moved and influenced by the Holy Spirit, Paul said, "This know also, that in the last days perilous times shall come" (2 Timothy 3:1). When we incorporate the original Greek meaning of the words in this verse, here is the *Renner Interpretive Version* (*RIV*) of Second Timothy 3:1:

> **You emphatically and categorically need to know with unquestionable certainty that in the very end of days — when time has sailed to its last port and no more time remains for the journey — that last season will stand in the midst of uncontrollable, unpredictable, hurtful, treacherous, and menacing times that will be emotionally difficult for people to bear.**

This is the Holy Spirit's prophetic preface to shake us and wake us to attention as He begins to unpack, through Paul, 25 specific dysfunctions that will be widespread throughout society in the last of the last days.

The First Seven Characteristics of the Last-Days Society

With pinpoint accuracy, Paul peered 2,000 years into the future and prophesied the sweeping signs we will see happening simultaneously at the end of the age. In verse 2, he said:

For men shall be lovers of their own selves, covetous, boasters, proud, blasphemers, disobedient to parents, unthankful, unholy.

— 2 Timothy 3:2

As we have noted, this passage begins with the Greek word *esontai* — translated here as "shall be." *Esontai* is from the word *eimi*, which means *I am*. Here, the Holy Spirit is giving us a major clue that at the end of the age, the world will become so self-absorbed, it will be known as the *I am* generation. The greatest priority in each person's life will be himself.

The next word we see is the Greek word *gar*, which is translated as "for" and serves as a conjunction that connects the "perilous times" referred to in verse 1 with the description of what those times will be like.

The word *gar* is followed by the phrase *hoi anthrōpoi*, which is translated as the word "men." The word *anthrōpoi* is the plural form of *anthropos*, which is the term for *man*, but when it is coupled with *hoi* and becomes *hoi anthrōpoi*, it describes *mankind at large*. The fact that these words are plural indicates that what is going to happen will be widespread and not confined to a few individuals. At the very end of the age, mankind will become…

#1 — Lovers of Their Own Selves

This is the chief characteristic of the last-days society. This phrase "lovers of their own selves" is a translation of the Greek word *philautoi*, which is the plural form of *philautos*, a compound of the words *philos* and *autos*. The word *philos* means *to love or to be fond of*, and it denotes *the love, fondness, attraction, or romantic feelings one has for another*. The word *autos* describes *oneself*. When compounded, the word *philautos* denotes an *unhealthy, inordinate love of self*.

Although there's nothing wrong with having a healthy love for oneself, this term is referring to people who are obsessed with themselves to the point of being *self-consumed*. They are so blinded by their own needs and wants, they're unable to see the needs of others. This *inordinate self-love* and *self-preoccupation* leads to mankind becoming…

#2 — Covetous

In Greek, the word "covetous" is *philargyroi*, which is from the words *philos* and *arguros*. Again, *philos* refers to *love, fondness, attraction*, and *romance* — and the word *arguros* is the word for *silver, money,* or *material possessions*. When compounded, *philargyroi* depicts *an inordinate love of or an abnormal preoccupation with money or material possessions.*

When a person is the center of his own universe (*philautos*), he is going to use his money and resources to take care of himself. This word *philargyroi* was used in ancient times to describe people who had an abundance of money and could have easily helped someone else, but they refused to do so because they were so fixated on satisfying their own needs and wants. This term describes *greediness* and consumerism on a scale that is out of control. All this is embodied in the Greek word *philarguros*. Next to arise will be…

#3 — Boasters

The word "boasters" is a translation of the Greek word *alazones*, the plural form of the word *alazon*. Again, this word denotes *one so committed to his own self-promotion and personal agenda that he is willing to exaggerate, overstate the facts, stretch the truth, embellish a story, and even lie if it will have a positive effect on his position or situation.* Essentially, this is *situational ethics* — when people flip-flop on morals, changing their positions to preserve their best interests and get ahead. They will willingly say or do anything if it will get them what they want.

One of the best examples of "boasters" in today's world is politicians. They often change their stories and their stance on issues, depending on what their constituents want to hear. This *floating ethical code* is a major sign of the very end of the age.

#4 — Proud

The fourth characteristic the apostle Paul forecasted we would see is a society that is *proud*. This is the Greek word *huperephanoi*, which is a compound of the words *huper* and *phanoi*. The word *huper* means *above* and depicts *a position of superiority*. And the word *phanoi*, which is the plural form of the word *phanos*, means *to be manifested*. When compounded to form *huperephanoi*, it describes *a person who sees himself above the rest of the crowd*. He is *arrogant, haughty, high-and-mighty, snooty, impudent, and insolent*.

Those that are "proud" believe themselves to be *the upper crust of society and intellectually advantaged above others*. In their minds, this gives them the right to dictate to everyone else what to believe and not believe. They consider themselves to be the trend-setters, and they seek to "cancel" anyone who disagrees with their ideology. This is precisely what this word *huperephanoi* means.

#5 — Blasphemers

Accompanied by the proud are who the Bible calls "blasphemers." In Greek, this is the word *blasphēmoi*, which is the plural form of the word *blasphemos*, and it basically describes *crude*, *rude*, or *vulgar language* — or *behavior*. Concerning language, it signifies *profane, foul, unclean words* and can refer to *blaspheming the divine*, but in general, it is *any derogatory speech intended to defame, injure, or harm another's reputation*. Regarding behavior, it refers to any *ungodly, debased, shameful actions* that go against the Word of God.

We're living in a world where the courts, the schools, and the entertainment industry are propagandizing all kinds of lifestyle choices that are contrary to Scripture. Things that were once considered blasphemous are now regularly paraded in front of us and celebrated. Those who disagree with such behaviors are mocked, ridiculed, and labeled as outcasts. This, too, the Holy Spirit warned us about in advance.

#6 — Disobedient to Parents

A society that is exceedingly self-absorbed and infatuated with itself will also produce children who are "disobedient to parents." This phrase in Greek is *goneusin apeithes*. The word *goneusin* means *to parents*, and the word *apeithes* is a form of the Greek word *peitho*, which means *to persuade* or *to convince*. However, when an "a" is added to the front and it becomes *apeithes*, the original meaning is cancelled. Thus, the word *apeithes* means *unpersuadable, uncontrollable,* or *unleadable*. In this condition, parents are *no longer able to persuade, control, lead,* or *exercise authority over* their children.

Shockingly, even our schools today are in support of children being disobedient to parents. More and more officials seem to be telling kids things like, "You don't have to do what your parents say or believe what they believe. You're in charge of your own life and your own destiny, and you shouldn't allow your parents to enforce rules or doctrines of faith that you don't agree with."

Some schools are even attempting to transition children from one gender to another without informing parents. This is an all-out assault on parenthood, which is what the Holy Spirit prophesied would take place at the very end of the last days.

#7 — Unthankful

Another major sign the apostle Paul identified is *unthankfulness*. This is a translation of the Greek word *acharistoi*, which is the plural form of the word *acharistos*. This word comes from the word *charis*, the term for *grace* in the New Testament. When *charis* becomes *charistos*, it denotes a *thankful, grateful, and appreciative attitude*. However, when an "a" is attached to the front of it and it becomes *acharistos*, the meaning is reversed. In this case, it changes the meaning to *unthankful, ungrateful, or unappreciative*.

The word *acharistoi* — translated here as "unthankful" — tells us that a thankful attitude previously prevailed, but now this person or group of people has *lost* its thankful, grateful, appreciative attitude and has replaced it with a sense of *entitlement*. Society at the end of the age will believe it is *entitled* to everything, and this "entitlement mentality" will be a societal ill in the last-days *I am* generation.

An entitlement mentality focuses on *taking*, not *giving*. This is the pinnacle of covetousness, which Paul mentioned in his list of end-times conditions. People who believe they are entitled to everything aren't thankful for anything. Sadly, in recent years, people in Western nations have been groomed to live under *a system of entitlement* and benefits at the government and taxpayers' expense.

Those who live with a sense of entitlement base their beliefs on how they *feel* — even if it doesn't match reality. For example, some young adults may *feel* unfairly treated if they're not able to start out with a lifestyle that it took their parents 30 years to achieve. Nevertheless, they feel entitled to it. Likewise, someone may *feel* they have a right to material possessions that others had to work very hard to attain. Although this thinking is unrealistic, entitled people believe they deserve it, and if they don't get it, they're angry with those who have it.

Moreover, someone may *feel* they have a right to a life filled with nonstop excitement, and when their life seems dull and boring, they feel deprived. Friend, this is a description of the day in which we're living. It is what the Holy Spirit prophesied would take place at the very end of the age. People in society who were once thankful and appreciative will begin to embrace an attitude of ingratitude and entitlement.

Where There Is Unthankfulness, 'Unholiness' Is Sure To Follow

Looking once more at Second Timothy 3:2, we read, "For men shall be lovers of their own selves, covetous, boasters, proud, blasphemers, disobedient to parents, unthankful, *unholy.*" This lets us know that where there is *unthankfulness, unholiness* is right behind it. The word "unholy" here is the Greek word *anosioi*, which is the plural form of the word *anosios.* This term is derived from the word *hosios*, which depicts *a person (or group of people) that is reverent, respectful, and God-fearing.* However, when an "a" is attached to the front of it, it has a cancelling effect.

Hence, the word *anosios* means that which was once holy has become *unholy*. Likewise, that which was once reverent has become *irreverent*, and that which was once respectful and God-fearing has become *disrespectful* and *no longer fears the Lord.* The word "unholy" depicts *those who have lost a fear of God and whose way of thinking and outward actions have become ill-mannered, impure, unclean, lewd, indecent, crude, coarse, vulgar, offensive, and rude.*

Moreover, it pictures an individual — or a group of people or even entire nations — who once revered and honored what was holy, sacred, and pure. But instead of revering things that are holy and sacred, their *thinking* and *behavior* became supportive of behaviors that are *unholy, unsacred,* and *impure.* This word "unholy" can actually describe thinking, behavior — activities or actions — that are *ill-mannered, improper, unclean, indecent, coarse, vulgar, offensive, crude, lewd, and rude* in the sight of God.

An end-times society will become *unthankful* and *unholy — impure, filthy, and filled with smut.* This is precisely what is happening in our times. One evening of TV can quickly show you that things impure, ill-mannered, improper, unclean, indecent, coarse, vulgar, offensive, crude, lewd, and rude are dominating the airwaves and affecting society in an unholy way. What was once considered *vulgar* and *immoral* is now widely accepted as appropriate. *These are all signs of the very last days.*

Could you have ever imagined that we would live in a world where society would go from praying at the beginning of the school day every day to outlawing references to God in school? Or that public recognition of God in educational institutions could result in legal action? Or that significant scriptures would become labeled as "hate speech"?

Did you ever think you'd see the day when small-business owners who refuse to do business with organizations that violate their personal convictions would be dragged into court and sued? Or that private business owners who use their own hard-earned profits to support Christian-based organizations would be sued because of where they choose to give their support? We are living in a day where freedom of religion has become freedom *from* religion.

Putting the meanings of all these words together, here is the *Renner Interpretive Version* (*RIV*) for Second Timothy 3:2:

> **Men will be self-focused, self-centered, self-absorbed, self-consumed, and in love with themselves more than anyone else. As a result of this self-love, they will be driven to obtain more and more and more. These boasters are so committed to their own agenda that they are willing to exaggerate, overstate the facts, stretch the truth, embellish a story, and even lie if it will get them the position, advantage, or goal they desire. They are arrogant, haughty, impudent, snooty, and insolent. They disdain, mock, slander, and speak ill of anyone who stands in the way of their ideology, and they freely use foul language. In this climate, parents will no longer be able to persuade, control, lead, or exercise authority over their own children. And although people were once thankful and appreciative, they will generally become void of gratitude and unappreciative of everything. Impurity will seep into society and cause it to become impure, ill-mannered, unclean, indecent, coarse, vulgar, offensive, crude, lewd, and rude.**

In our next lesson, we will turn our attention to the next item on Paul's list of last-days characteristics — the breakdown of family and relationships.

Questions and Answers With Rick Renner

In the program, Rick answered the following question from one of our viewers.

Q. What is a "false prophet"?

A. In New Testament writings, the rise of *false prophets* in the last days is mentioned. The word "false" is from the Greek word *pseudes*, and it describes *something that is false or bogus*. It can also depict *someone who is an imposter*. The word "prophets" in Greek is *prophetes*, and it basically describes *one who speaks on behalf of God*.

When these words are joined to form the phrase "false prophets" — *pseudes prophetes* — it describes *one who is a pretender*. This is a person who *pretends* to be a prophet. Hence, this phrase could be translated as *a bogus prophet* or *a charlatan prophet*. What is interesting is that this individual may have started as a genuine prophet, but somewhere along the way, the person became fraudulent in his or her activities and therefore they became *a bogus prophet*.

(For in-depth teaching on the subject of false prophets and how to determine the fake ones from the real ones, we suggest securing a copy of Rick's book or series entitled *Apostles and Prophets — Their Roles in the Past, the Present, and the Last Days*.)

STUDY QUESTIONS

> Study to shew thyself approved unto God, a workman that needeth not to be ashamed, rightly dividing the word of truth.
> — 2 Timothy 2:15

1. *Unholiness* is a condition that comes on gradually. Once *unthankfulness* begins to take root in a person's heart, little by little he or she becomes more and more irreverent, disrespectful, and impure. Be honest. Does this describe you? Have you developed a *casual attitude* toward words, attitudes, and actions that are *unholy, impure,* and *unsanctioned by God*? Are you losing your fear of the Lord?

2. One of the most important qualities we can and should pray for is a healthy reverential *fear of God*. The Bible is filled with references to the benefits this virtue brings. Take time to reflect on these passages — writing down what the fear of the Lord is and how it blesses your life.

   - Deuteronomy 10:12
   - Psalm 25:12-14; 33:6-8,18,19; 34:7,9,11-14; 111:1
   - Proverbs 1:7; 2:1-5; 8:13; 9:10; 10:27; 14:26,27; 16:6; 19:23; 22:4
   - Ecclesiastes 12:13

PRACTICAL APPLICATION

> But be ye doers of the word, and not hearers only,
> deceiving your own selves.
> —James 1:22

1. It has been said that what we *behold* we *become*, which is one reason why David declared, "I will set no wicked thing before mine eyes…" (Psalm 101:3). Without question, today's movies, music, and television programming are filled with unholy images and messages. Is there anything the Holy Spirit is bringing to mind that you have been watching and listening to that is grieving His heart? If so, what is it?

2. What changes do you need to make in your life to guard yourself and your family from that which is unholy and unclean? What do you need to eliminate to keep your mind and heart pure? How can you be more pleasing to the Lord who loves you so much?

LESSON 8

TOPIC
The Breakdown of Family and Relationships

SCRIPTURES

2 Timothy 3:1-3 — This know also, that in the last days perilous times shall come. For men shall be lovers of their own selves, covetous, boasters, proud, blasphemers, disobedient to parents, unthankful, unholy, without natural affection, trucebreakers, false accusers, incontinent, fierce, despisers of those that are good.

GREEK WORDS

1. "without natural affection"— ἄστοργος (*astorgos*): from στοργος (*storgos*), a devotion and commitment to one's family; but an ἄ (a) is added to the word; therefore, it depicts a lack of devotion to family;

an absence of commitment to one's family; the deterioration of family relationships; the loss of family affection
2. "trucebreakers" — **ἄσπονδος** (*aspondos*): from **σπονδος** (*spondos*), which means to make a covenant; but when an **ἄ** (*a*) is added to the word, it means to undo a covenant, or pictures one who breaks a covenant; thus, covenant-breaking is used to picture divorce; literally, irreconcilable differences resulting in the breaking of a covenant
3. "false accusers" — **διάβολος** (*diabolos*): most often translated as "devil"; slanderer; accuser; used in 2 Timothy 3:3 to depict a court system overrun with lawsuits

SYNOPSIS

Have you ever heard of *the domino effect*? It is a phrase that was first used in the 1920s, describing a snowball effect that takes place when one event initiates a chain of similar events that happen one after another. In many ways, the prophetic signs of what society will experience in the last of the last days are much the same. Each characteristic is built upon the previous one, and once they begin to fall into place, there's no stopping them. Indeed, the breakdown of the family — which is the next end-time sign Paul listed — will trigger a series of related troubles that we need to be aware of and take measures to guard against.

The emphasis of this lesson:

The Holy Spirit prophesied that at the very end of the age, there would be a breakdown of the traditional family, and due to irreconcilable differences, an epidemic of divorce will occur. This deterioration of relationships will give way to an overloaded court system where people will default to suing each other rather than working out their disagreements.

A Review of Second Timothy 3:1,2
The *Renner Interpretive Version* (*RIV*)

There is so much that we have learned so far from **Second Timothy 3:1 and 2**. Before we move on to verse 3, let's take another look at the *Renner Interpretive Version* (*RIV*) of verses 1 and 2:

> **You emphatically and categorically need to know with unquestionable certainty that in the very end of days — when time has sailed**

to its last port and no more time remains for the journey — that last season will stand in the midst of uncontrollable, unpredictable, hurtful, treacherous, and menacing times that will be emotionally difficult for people to bear.

Men will be self-focused, self-centered, self-absorbed, self-consumed, and in love with themselves more than anyone else. As a result of this self-love, they will be driven to obtain more and more and more. These boasters are so committed to their own agenda that they are willing to exaggerate, overstate the facts, stretch the truth, embellish a story, and even lie if it will get them the position, advantage, or goal they desire. They are arrogant, haughty, impudent, snooty, and insolent. They disdain, mock, slander, and speak ill of anyone who stands in the way of their ideology, and they freely use foul language. In this climate, parents will no longer be able to persuade, control, lead, or exercise authority over their own children. And although people were once thankful and appreciative, they will generally become void of gratitude and unappreciative of everything. Impurity will seep into society and cause it to become impure, ill-mannered, unclean, indecent, coarse, vulgar, offensive, crude, lewd, and rude.

Isn't it amazing to uncover all the rich treasures of meaning found within the original Greek text! These two verses are laden with truth and they help us understand a great deal of what the Holy Spirit prophesied would take place in the last of the last days. Armed with this understanding, we can more successfully navigate these times and not fall prey to the spirit of the age. Now let's turn our attention to Second Timothy 3:3 and see what else the Spirit said we can expect in these final hours.

The World Will Be 'Without Natural Affection'

As Paul continued to write under the powerful influence of the Holy Spirit, he prophesied that the majority of people in the last days would become "without natural affection, trucebreakers, false accusers, incontinent, fierce, despisers of those that are good" (2 Timothy 3:3).

Notice the words "without natural affection." This is a translation of the Greek word *astorgoi*, which is the plural form of *astorgos*. It is from the word *storgos*, which describes *a devotion and commitment to one's family*. In this case, however, an "a" is added to the front of the word, cancelling or reversing its meaning. Therefore, the word *astorgos* depicts *a lack of devotion to family* or *an absence of commitment to one's family*. It can also mean *the deterioration of family relationships* or *the loss of family affection*.

By using this word *astorgos*, the Holy Spirit was prophesying through Paul that at the very end of the age, there would be a breakdown and deterioration of the traditional family and the home. This word depicts individuals who have drifted so far apart that they reached the point of *irreconcilable differences*. Consequently, they found it easier to part ways than work to stay together.

Without question, if you look across society today, marriages and families are under attack. It is taking place all around us in epic proportions. Some of the common causes for this dreadful deterioration of the family include:

- Traditional family relationships are threatened by over-busy schedules, financial pressures, and people living in one home, each trying to hold down a job.
- There are multiple cars, multiple televisions, multiple digital devices, and everyone going in different directions.
- Parents are going in one direction, while children go in another direction; and often, even dads and moms aren't going in the same direction.
- The family resides in one house, but they do not share life together. Often they don't even share a meal together.

Sociologists say these factors have contributed to rebellion in children who feel neglected. They have also led to disorders in children who are rushed from one place to the next. Add to this a deterioration of marriages due to such fast-paced lifestyles that husbands and wives don't regularly take time to connect. The Holy Spirit said the breakdown of the family and home is a sign of the very end of the age, and the reason He warned us about it is so that we would not fall victim to it.

'Truce-Breaking' Will Abound

The breakdown and deterioration of family relationships and the loss of family affection logically leads to the next dysfunction in society, which Paul identifies as "trucebreakers" (*see* 2 Timothy 3:3). In Greek, this is the word *aspondoi*, which is the plural form of *aspondos*. It is taken from the word *spondos*, which means *to make a covenant*. However, when an "*a*" is added to the front, it has a canceling effect. Thus, the word *aspondos* means *to undo a covenant*, or pictures *one who breaks a covenant*. This means we could translate the word "trucebreakers" in the *King James Version* as *covenant-breakers*.

It's interesting to note that the word *aspondos* is the very word the Greeks used to describe the idea of *irreconcilable differences*. The use of this term in this passage lets us know that at the very end of the age, a season will arise in which individuals in covenant relationships will drift apart until they reach a point of *irreconcilable differences* between themselves. Hence, the word *aspondos* is literally used to picture *divorce*. In the last of the last days, mankind will experience a pandemic of divorce.

There is no judgment for anyone who has gone through a divorce. Clearly, there are some marital situations that cannot be fixed because both parties must be willing to humble themselves and sacrifice their needs and desires to see the relationship healed. Nevertheless, at the very end of the age — when society is saturated with inordinate, unhealthy self-love — people will choose to divorce and walk away rather than stay and work on reconciling.

Of course, there are other types of covenants that people will easily break, which means the word *aspondos* can also refer to *the breaking of a covenant between two close friends, the breaking of a covenant between an individual and his church*, or *the breaking of a covenant between two or more business partners*. Sadly, a handshake over an agreement is no longer a guarantee that a commitment will be kept. Again, the Holy Spirit prophesied that this act of covenant-breaking will run rampant in the last of the last days.

Our Court System Will Be Overloaded

The exponential increase in covenant-breakers will provide the perfect conditions for the next wave of societal dysfunction, which the Bible identifies as "false accusers." This is a translation of the Greek word *diaboloi*. It is from the word *diabolos*, which is most often translated as "devil" in the New Testament, and it means *slanderer* or *accuser*.

Strangely, the word *diaboloi* used in Second Timothy 3:3 depicts the devil getting into the court system and that *court system being overrun with lawsuits*. The Holy Spirit uses this word to tell us that in the very end of the age, society will feel as though the devil himself has been released with full force into the judicial system. In a world where everyone is in love with themselves and solely concerned with his own needs, slander and accusations will be flying left and right, and people will default to going to court and suing one another rather than choosing to sit down and work out their disagreements.

Clearly, we are living in a day when the devil is in the court system — weaponizing the law to accuse, attack, slander, vilify, and ravage others financially. The ability and willingness to negotiate, come to terms, or settle disagreements in a civilized way have been virtually lost. In today's culture, shoppers sue store owners, employees sue employers, patients sue doctors, parents sue schools, and children even sue parents. Although there are times when filing a lawsuit and going to court is the only course of action, as believers, we should try to take a different route first.

So when Paul prophesied that there would be a rise of "false accusers" — the Greek word *diaboloi* — at the very end of the age, he was putting us on notice that the practice of *accusing* and being *accused* would get so out of control that it would seem as if *the devil himself* had infiltrated the courts and released his fury.

It is remarkable how each word used in Second Timothy 3 is built one upon the next. It's clear to see how the breakdown of the home — *astorgoi* — results in covenant breaking or divorce, which is what the word *aspondoi* means. Similarly, we can see how covenant breaking or divorce gives way to "false accusers" (*diabloi*) — where the devil has fallen into the court system, and it becomes overrun with lawsuits.

Taking into account the original Greek meaning, here is the *Renner Interpretive Version* (*RIV*) of the first part of Second Timothy 3:3:

> **Love for and commitment to family will disintegrate, and divorce will become epidemic, with irreconcilable differences being a major factor in tearing families apart. In fact, every imaginable type of covenant will be regularly violated, and the court system will be overwhelmed as people go overboard, suing and being sued….**

Look how accurate the Holy Spirit was in describing the end of the age! Again, His purpose in telling us these things is not to scare us but to prepare us so that we don't become a statistic of these things which will ransack society in the last of the last days.

Questions and Answers With Rick Renner

In the program, Rick answered the following question from one of our viewers.

Q. Who is the worst member of the church?

A. The answer is found in **James 3:5 and 6**, where the Bible says:

> **Even so the tongue is a little member, and boasteth great things. Behold, how great a matter a little fire kindleth!**
>
> **And the tongue is a fire, a world of iniquity: so is the tongue among our members, that it defileth the whole body, and setteth on fire the course of nature; and it is set on fire of hell.**

Hands down, the tongue is the worst member of any church because if the tongue is not brought under the control of the Holy Spirit, it will say what it should not say. It will murmur and complain about anything it doesn't like and offer its negative opinion about what it has no right to be talking about. Left unchecked, the tongue gossips, slanders, and accuses others, starting fires that are hard to extinguish.

Indeed, the tongue is the worst member of any church, which is why we need to surrender it to the control of the Holy Spirit. The Spirit is the only One who is able to tame the tongue and harness its power to be a source of blessing instead of cursing.

STUDY QUESTIONS

> Study to shew thyself approved unto God, a workman that needeth not to be ashamed, rightly dividing the word of truth.
> — 2 Timothy 2:15

1. Having "natural affection" — the Greek word *storgos* — is a devotion and commitment to one's family. In your own words, describe what devotion and commitment to your family looks like in a practical sense and a spiritual sense. As you answer, consider Paul's instructions in First Timothy 5:8 and Galatians 6:9,10.

2. According to Hebrews 13:4 and Jesus' words in Matthew 19:4-6, how important and precious is marriage in God's eyes? Have you placed this same value on your marriage? What practical steps can you take to make your relationship with your mate a higher priority? (*See* Ephesians 5:21-33.)

3. Who does Revelation 12:9 and 10 identify as the "accuser of the brethren"? So if you are hearing thoughts of accusation about your spouse, your children, your pastor, or anyone else, where are they coming from? If you listen to, accept, and then verbalize the accusations, who are you acting like and working for?

4. Instead of accusing and criticizing those who disappoint and offend you, what does First Peter 3:8-12 say that God wants you to do? (Also consider Jesus' words in Matthew 5:43-45.)

PRACTICAL APPLICATION

> But be ye doers of the word, and not hearers only, deceiving your own selves.
> —James 1:22

1. From your vantage point, what are some examples of the deterioration of the traditional family that you have personally witnessed? What disturbs you most about these? (Consider things the mainstream media is producing, things happening in and around your community, as well as events in the lives of families you know.)

2. Does life for you and your family seem to be overcrowded and moving at breakneck speed? Press "pause" on your life and pray: "Lord, are there any activities or commitments in my life that I need to discontinue? Is there something I'm involved in that You're done with — something that was once life-giving but is now dead and weighing me down?" Be still and listen. What is the Holy Spirit speaking to you about your schedule? What actions is He prompting you to take?

3. Some practices that help unite families and strengthen family ties include having meals together, going on a vacation, playing games, attending church together, praying together, and reading God's Word together (having brief devotionals). What other things can you think of doing to promote family unity? What adjustments can you make in your routine to incorporate one or more of these life-giving activities?

LESSON 9

TOPIC
Widespread Violence

SCRIPTURES
2 Timothy 3:1-3 — This know also, that in the last days perilous times shall come. For men shall be lovers of their own selves, covetous, boasters, proud, blasphemers, disobedient to parents, unthankful, unholy, without natural affection, trucebreakers, false accusers, incontinent, fierce, despisers of those that are good.

GREEK WORDS
1. "incontinent" — ἀκρατής (*akrates*): the inability to exercise control; a lack of control; a lack of self-restraint; the inability to say no
2. "fierce" — ἀνήμερος (*anemeros*): savage or uncivilized; from a root word that pictures people who are gentle, kind, or mild, but the form of this word pictures those who are harsh, cruel, savage, vicious, or violent
3. "despisers of those that are good" — ἀφιλάγαθος (*aphilagathos*): pictures a hater of that which is good; a strange word that in its oldest and truest sense depicts a society where the law is not primarily intended to protect the rights of good people; rather, the law is intended to protect the rights of offenders; a word so unusual that it is only used once in the New Testament

SYNOPSIS
Jesus declared, "As it was in the days of Noah, so it will be at the coming of the Son of Man" (Matthew 24:37 *NIV*). According to Genesis 6, the days of Noah were filled with *violence* (*see* vv. 11,13). Clearly, the world we live in is saturated with violence. From the violence and brutality of man against man and country against country to the simulated carnage in movies, television, and video games — widespread violence is all around us. But just because the world is caught in a whirlwind of savagery doesn't mean we have to be. With the wisdom and strength of the Holy Spirit,

we can learn to navigate these last days victoriously and be ready for His return!

The emphasis of this lesson:

Three additional telltale signs that we have arrived at the last of the last days is that society will become incontinent, fierce, and despisers of those that are good. This means people will lack self-control, embrace cruelty and violence, and establish laws that protect the rights of offenders more than the rights of good people.

A Review of Second Timothy 3:1,2
The *Renner Interpretive Version* (*RIV*)

Writing under the inspiration of the Holy Spirit, the apostle Paul prophesied what we can expect to see taking place in society at the very end of the age. He declared, "This know also, that in the last days perilous times shall come. For men shall be lovers of their own selves, covetous, boasters, proud, blasphemers, disobedient to parents, unthankful, unholy" (2 Timothy 3:1,2).

We have meticulously unpacked these verses in our previous lessons and discovered the original Greek meaning. Here again is the *Renner Interpretive Version* (*RIV*) of Second Timothy 3:1 and 2:

> You emphatically and categorically need to know with unquestionable certainty that in the very end of days — when time has sailed to its last port and no more time remains for the journey — that last season will stand in the midst of uncontrollable, unpredictable, hurtful, treacherous, and menacing times that will be emotionally difficult for people to bear.
>
> Men will be self-focused, self-centered, self-absorbed, self-consumed, and in love with themselves more than anyone else. As a result of this self-love, they will be driven to obtain more and more and more. These boasters are so committed to their own agenda that they are willing to exaggerate, overstate the facts, stretch the truth, embellish a story, and even lie if it will get them the position, advantage, or goal they desire. They are arrogant, haughty, impudent, snooty, and insolent. They disdain, mock, slander, and speak ill of anyone who stands in

the way of their ideology, and they freely use foul language. In this climate, parents will no longer be able to persuade, control, lead, or exercise authority over their own children. And although people were once thankful and appreciative, they will generally become void of gratitude and unappreciative of everything. Impurity will seep into society and cause it to become impure, ill-mannered, unclean, indecent, coarse, vulgar, offensive, crude, lewd, and rude.

The Holy Spirit in His infinite wisdom foretold these things so we would be proactive in building our lives on the unshakable foundation of God's Word and avoid being swept up in this end-times' pandemonium. Before we move further into this lesson, let's review what we learned from Second Timothy 3:3 in our last lesson.

Mankind Will Be 'Without Natural Affection, Trucebreakers, and False Accusers'

As Paul continued painting a prophetic picture of the last of the last days, he went on to say that people in society would be "without natural affection, trucebreakers, false accusers, incontinent, fierce, despisers of those that are good" (2 Timothy 3:3).

"**Without natural affection**" is a translation of the Greek word *astorgoi*, which is the plural form of the word *astorgos*. It is from the word *storgos*, which describes *a devotion and commitment to one's family*. However, because an "a" is added to the front of the word, it cancels or reverses the meaning. Thus, the word *astorgos* denotes *a lack of devotion to family* or *an absence of commitment to one's family*. It can also mean *the deterioration of family relationships* or *the loss of family affection*.

By using this word *astorgoi*, the Holy Spirit is telling us that at the very end of the age, there will be a breakdown and deterioration of the traditional family and the home. Families will have drifted so far apart that they will reach the point of *irreconcilable differences*. As a result, it will seem easier to part ways than to work to stay together.

Friend, we're seeing this take place before our very eyes. Traditional family relationships are threatened by over-crowded schedules, financial pressures, and more than one job in a home — not to mention multiple cars, multiple televisions, multiple digital devices, etc. Although these may seem to be a blessing, they can create separate paths for family members — paths that rarely converge — if they're not properly managed.

Indeed, just about everything that could cause a family to drift apart is taking place in families today. Life seems to be moving at breakneck speed, and while the family resides together in one house, they simply don't share life together. The Holy Spirit is alerting us to the issue so that we will take preventative measures and guard our family so that it doesn't become part of the statistics.

"Trucebreakers" is the second group of people Paul mentioned in Second Timothy 3:3, and it is the Greek word *aspondoi*, the plural form of *aspondos*. This word is taken from the word *spondos*, which means *to make a covenant*. However, because an *"a"* has been added to the front, it's meaning is cancelled. Hence, the word *aspondos* means *to undo a covenant* or *to break a covenant*. The fact that the word is plural in this passage (*aspondoi*) means *a widespread pandemic of divorce* will occur at the end of the age.

So in addition to the breakdown of the family, we also see a breakdown in marriages. Interestingly, the word *aspondos* is the very term the Greeks used to describe the idea of *irreconcilable differences*, and these irreconcilable differences are not limited to the covenant between husbands and wives. At the end of the age, covenants will be broken between close friends, between business partners, and between individuals and their church.

Clearly today, fewer and fewer people actually take their covenants and promises seriously. The Holy Spirit warned that in the last of the last days this issue of covenant breaking would become widespread. By God's grace we can learn how to be proactive in our relationships and guard ourselves from this pitfall.

"False accusers" is the next type of depravation Paul listed. These words are a translation of the Greek word *diaboloi*, which is the plural form of the word *diabolos*. In the New Testament, the word *diabolos* is most often translated as "devil," and it means *slanderer* or *accuser*. When *diabolos* becomes *diaboloi* as it does in Second Timothy 3:3, it depicts *a court system that is overrun with accusations, slander, liable, and lawsuits*.

The Holy Spirit uses this word to tell us that in the last of the last days, society will feel as though the devil himself has been released with full force into the judicial system. Rather than choosing to sit down and work through their disagreements in a civilized way, people will default to going to court and suing one another.

Friend, we are seeing this take place daily. The devil is in the court system — weaponizing the law to accuse, attack, slander, vilify, and ravage others financially. Paul used the word *diaboloi* — translated here as "false accusers" — to forewarn us that the practice of *accusing* and being *accused* will get so out of control it will seem as if *the devil himself* has infiltrated the courts and released his fury.

People Will Be Unable To Control Themselves

What else did Paul say about people living at the end of the age? He said they would be "incontinent" (*see* 2 Timothy 3:3). When most people hear this word, they automatically think of the medical condition in which a person has lost control of his or her bladder or bowels. In this verse, however, it describes *the inability to exercise control*.

This word "incontinent" is the Greek word *akrates*, which is the plural form of *akratos*, and it is derived from the word *kratos*, the term meaning *power* or *to be in power*. Again, we see the letter "a" has been added to the front of *kratos*, transforming it into the word *akratos*, which cancels or reverses the meaning. So rather than one having power, *akratos* describes *a lack of power or control* or *a lack of self-restraint*. It carries the idea of *one who is unable to say no*.

This is a picture of a person or a society that has lost the ability to control itself and has abandoned self-restraint. Hence, the word "incontinent" — from the Greek word *akrates* — perfectly describes a person or a group of people who live with an "I just can't say no" mindset that ultimately leads to destruction because it produces life with few boundaries and restraints.

Because the word "incontinent" refers to those who have lost self-control and lack willpower, it could depict:

- A person who has *no ability to stop eating*.
- A person who has *no ability to stop spending*.
- A person who has *no ability to restrain emotions*.
- A person who has *no ability to stop addictive behaviors*.

People who have lost their restraint when it comes to eating often end up obese and battling various types of disorders and diseases. Those who have lost control of their spending often end up in debt with maxed-out credit cards and enslaved to their lenders. And people who have lost their ability to control their emotions often experience broken relationships, deep inner wounds, and social isolation. Just think of the fallout from issues like road rage, domestic abuse, and incivility in the workplace.

The truth of the matter is, an inability to control oneself in any area of one's life affects every area of one's life. This is especially true with addictive behaviors, which are at an all-time high. Today, more people are addicted to things like alcohol, drugs, pornography, gambling, and sex than ever before. The Holy Spirit prophesied through Paul that people in the last days would become "incontinent," lacking self-control and self-restraint, and that is exactly what we are seeing.

Society Will Become 'Fierce'

The next dysfunctional trait Paul said we would see in society is that people will be "fierce" (*see* 2 Timothy 3:3). This is the Greek word *anemeroi*, which is the plural form of *anemeros*. It is formed from the word *hemeros* — a word that means *civilized, cultivated, cultured, gentle, mild, polished, tame*, or *well-behaved*. However, when an "a" is added to the front and it becomes *anemeros*, it pictures a person who is *savage* or *uncivilized* — one who is *harsh, cruel, vicious*, or *violent*.

When most of us think of savage and barbaric acts in history, we often think of a tyrannical leader who tortured and slaughtered thousands of people. An example would be the ancient Roman Empire that carried out many vicious acts. In that particular period of history, Romans packed stadiums, such as the Colosseum, and watched with glee as unimaginable tortures and persecutions were carried out against criminals, especially early Christians who put their faith in the Lord Jesus. It seems that the crowds couldn't get enough of seeing blood spattered and spilt in the arenas below.

Today — at a time in modern history when we seem to be more highly sophisticated — we've taken the barbaric behavior of the ancient world to a new, unprecedented level. Although we may seem to be more sophisticated, the reality is we no longer have to visit stadiums and other venues to experience violence and bloodshed. Now we bring huge doses of it directly into our homes through television, digital devices, and the Internet.

Although the way in which we receive our entertainment may be more technologically advanced, this current generation is as barbaric, or even more so, than any previous generations. It's just barbarism manifesting in a different form. Consider these statistics:

- By age 18, a child will have seen more than 200,000 acts of violence on television and witnessed more than 40,000 simulated murders.

- The average seventh-grader watches more than four hours of television per day — with more than 60-percent of programs containing violence.

- The same average seventh-grader plays electronic games four hours per week — with more than 50-percent of games categorized as "violent."

- Between the seventh and twelfth grades, the average teenager now listens to more than 10,500 hours of music — much of which is violence-related.

This present generation has seen so much brutality on the screens in front of them that they have become numb to it. People purchase tickets to see movies filled with scenes of human slaughter and horrific behavior and violence play out in front of them. It's thrilling "entertainment" in their eyes, and it is the hottest-selling ticket at the movies.

Of course, we can't talk about violence in society without mentioning the issue of *abortion*, which is likely the number-one form of barbarism in our day. Global data confirms that between the years of 1980 and 2020 (40 years), nearly *2 billion abortions* have been carried out globally. Statistics estimate that 125,000 abortions are performed every day worldwide — a nauseating fact that deeply grieves the heart of God.

As society becomes more and more obsessed with images of violence, it is seeping into the mainstream. The Holy Spirit prophesied through Paul that fierce, cruel, violence — from the Greek word *anemeros* — would escalate at the very end of the age, and we are witnessing the prophetic fulfillment of this truth.

'Despisers of Those That Are Good'

Along with incontinent and fierce, the apostle Paul went on to say people will be "despisers of those that are good" (*see* 2 Timothy 3:3). This unique phrase is a translation of the Greek word *aphilagathoi*, which is the plural form of *aphilagathos* — a word that is taken from *philagathos*, a compound of the words *phileo* and *agathos*. Again, the word *phileo* means *to love* or *to have an affection for*, and the word *agathos* describes anything that is *good or beneficial*. When compounded to form the word *philagathos*, it describes *one that has an affinity for whatever is good, beneficial, and promotes one's well-being*.

But when an "a" is placed at the front, the meaning is cancelled or reversed. Thus, the word *aphilagathos* pictures *a hater of that which is good*. This strange word in its oldest and truest sense depicts a society where the law is *not* primarily intended to protect the rights of good people — rather, the law is intended to protect the rights of offenders. Instead of protecting upstanding, law-abiding citizens, the law protects those who are evil and immoral, often leaving good people with no defense. This word is so unusual, it is only used once in the New Testament.

It certainly does seem that we're living in a time when society fights to defend offenders and even makes excuses for them, while at the same time often leaving the rights of victims and good citizens in jeopardy. As ludicrous as this is, it shouldn't surprise us, because the Holy Spirit prophesied that we should expect this. It is one of the many signs that we have sailed to the very "last port" of this age, and little to no time remains on our journey.

Again, each of these characteristics — *incontinent, fierce*, and *despisers of those that are good* — are all plural in the Greek text, indicating that these conditions will not be isolated to certain individuals. Instead, they will be widespread and pandemic in proportion as we get closer and closer to the very end of the age.

Taking into account the original Greek meaning of the words we've studied, here is the *Renner Interpretive Version (RIV)* of Second Timothy 3:3:

> **Love for and commitment to family will disintegrate, and divorce will become epidemic, with irreconcilable differences being a major factor in tearing families apart. In fact, every imaginable type of covenant will be regularly violated, and the court system will be overwhelmed as people go overboard, suing and being sued. People will generally lose the ability to say no and will be unable to control their instincts in nearly every area of life. People will become savage, and it will eventually feel like there are no laws to protect the innocent.**

Although it seems our situation is very dark and desperate, it is not time for us to throw in the towel and give up. God has anointed us to live in these last of the last days and given us the greatest opportunity — and privilege — to share the Good News of Jesus Christ and to help bring in a last-days harvest of souls before the age concludes. It's time to take hold of all the spiritual weapons God has provided and begin to daily live, with purpose, on our mission! If you will do what you can do, the Spirit of God will do what you can't do. He will faithfully guard and keep you until the very end!

Questions and Answers With Rick Renner

In the program, Rick answered the following question from one of our viewers.

Q. Did angels mate with earthly women in Old Testament times?

A. As bizarre as this sounds, the answer is *yes*. The Bible states that just before the Flood of Noah's day, certain angels — identified in Scripture as "sons of God" — abandoned their assigned positions of authority and rebelled against God. The Bible says:

> **And it came to pass, when men began to multiply on the face of the earth, and daughters were born unto them, that the sons of God saw the daughters of men that they were fair; and they took them wives of all which they chose.**
> **— Genesis 6:2**

Driven by lust for the daughters of mankind, certain angels who were assigned to protect, preserve, and assist humanity left their God-assigned positions, took on the form of men, and began to cohabit and have sexual relations with earthly women. What was the outcome of their illicit behavior? Scripture says:

> **There were giants in the earth in those days; and also after that, when the sons of God came in unto the daughters of men, and they bear children to them, the same became mighty men which were of old, men of renown.**
> **— Genesis 6:4**

Again, the "sons of God" are nefarious angels who rebelled against Him and began to crossbreed with earthly women, producing monstrous giants that brought great violence, wickedness, and corruption to the entire earth. The actions of these angels that sinned did not go unpunished (*see* 2 Peter 2:4; Jude 6). What's more, Jesus said what took place in the days of Noah is what we can expect to see in the last of the last days (*see* Matthew 24:37,38).

(To expand your understanding of what took place in the days of Noah with the nefarious angels who sinned, we recommend Rick's series *Fallen Angels, Giants, Monsters, and the World Before the Flood*.)

STUDY QUESTIONS

> Study to shew thyself approved unto God, a workman that needeth not to be ashamed, rightly dividing the word of truth.
> — 2 Timothy 2:15

1. *Incontinence* — the inability to exercise self-control or self-restraint — will rise sharply in the last days. However, as a child of God, you don't have to become enslaved by an undisciplined, out-of-control life. What does Philippians 4:13 say you are able to do? According to Galatians 5:16 and 22-25, where does self-control come from and what must you do to walk in it? (Also consider Romans 8:1-17.)
2. The hideous and barbaric loss of life through abortion is staggering. What does God think and say about the shedding of innocent blood in Proverbs 6:16,17; 24:11,12; and Isaiah 1:15? What practical and spiritual steps can you take to promote life and peace and help protect the blood of the innocent? (Also consider Proverbs 12:6; 31:8.)
3. Instead of cowering in fear at society's "fierceness," God wants you to rise up and follow Jesus' example. According to Jesus' words in Luke 10:19 and Matthew 16:19 and 18:18-20, what has He Himself given you? How does He want you to use it? In what ways can you more fully utilize and exercise what He's given you to bring light and life to the people in the world around you?

PRACTICAL APPLICATION

> But be ye doers of the word, and not hearers only, deceiving your own selves.
> — James 1:22

1. Be honest. How do you react when you see someone's life being taken in a movie or TV show? Is your reaction any different when you

hear about it in real life? Have you become desensitized to scenes of violence and bloodshed? Is murder and brutality normal to you? What changes is the Holy Spirit inspiring you to make in your and your family's personal media choices?

2. Are there areas in your life where you find it hard to exercise self-control — areas of wrong thinking or behavior that you just can't seem to say *no* to? If so, what are those areas?

3. Take time now to repent of any ungodly mindsets or habits you've been tolerating and ask the Holy Spirit to develop the fruit of *self-control* in your life. Using a Bible concordance — which is usually located in the back of your Bible — or an online search engine, find scriptures that address the areas of thinking and behavior you want to overcome. Look up key words that describe both the problem and the solution (the godly behavior you want to see in your life.) Write out and meditate on the verses the Holy Spirit brings alive to you.

4. What specific steps can you take to lessen the likelihood of falling back into wrong thinking or behavior? What people, places, or things do you need to stay away from? What godly alternatives can you begin including in your life to promote positive change?

LESSON 10

TOPIC
An End-Times Hurricane

SCRIPTURES
2 Timothy 3:1-3 — This know also, that in the last days perilous times shall come. For men shall be lovers of their own selves, covetous, boasters, proud, blasphemers, disobedient to parents, unthankful, unholy, without natural affection, trucebreakers, false accusers, incontinent, fierce, despisers of those that are good, traitors, heady, highminded, lovers of pleasures more than lovers of God.

GREEK WORDS
1. "traitors"— **προδότης** (*prodotes*): one who is a traitor to an oath; one who betrays or abandons a friend; a lack of commitment to oaths or relationships; one who is treacherous in the context of an oath or a relationship; a fair-weather friend
2. "heady"— **προπετής** (*propetes*): reckless; impulsive; it can depict people so wholly given to violence that they enjoy violence and become known for their violent, reckless, rash, emotional intemperance
3. "highminded"— **τυφόω** (*tuphoo*): to be inflated with pride; pictures one puffed up and clouded by his own sense of self-importance; it is where we get the word typhoon

SYNOPSIS
What do people do when they know a storm of hurricane proportions is heading their way? They *prepare*! Windows are boarded up; vehicles are moved to higher ground; and loved ones are taken out of harm's way. Anything that can be damaged or destroyed is packed up and secured ahead of the coming storm.

Spiritually, there is an end-time storm racing toward us. We can already see its bands on our radar, and we, too, must prepare ourselves, our family, and our loved ones. The good news is that just as hurricanes and typhoons blow in, they also blow out. As God's people, we must take the necessary precautions to weather the storm and then unite with like-minded people to rebuild spiritually once the storm has passed.

The emphasis of this lesson:

Traitorous, heady, and high-minded men and women will abound at the end of the age. These include people who are fair-weather friends, individuals who are reckless and impulsive, and those who are puffed up by a sense of their own self-importance.

A Review of Second Timothy 3:1-3
The *Renner Interpretive Version* (*RIV*)

Just before we begin our lesson, let's revisit what the apostle Paul prophesied more than 2,000 years ago regarding the condition of humanity in the last of the last days. Moved upon by the Holy Spirit Paul wrote,

"This know also, that in the last days perilous times shall come. For men shall be lovers of their own selves, covetous, boasters, proud, blasphemers, disobedient to parents, unthankful, unholy, without natural affection, trucebreakers, false accusers, incontinent, fierce, despisers of those that are good" (2 Timothy 3:1-3).

When we insert the original Greek meaning of the words in these verses, the passages come alive with a richer, more expanded understanding. Here is the *Renner Interpretive Version* (*RIV*) of Second Timothy 3:1-3:

> **You emphatically and categorically need to know with unquestionable certainty that in the very end of days — when time has sailed to its last port and no more time remains for the journey — that last season will stand in the midst of uncontrollable, unpredictable, hurtful, treacherous, and menacing times that will be emotionally difficult for people to bear.**
>
> **Men will be self-focused, self-centered, self-absorbed, self-consumed, and in love with themselves more than anyone else. As a result of this self-love, they will be driven to obtain more and more and more. These boasters are so committed to their own agenda that they are willing to exaggerate, overstate the facts, stretch the truth, embellish a story, and even lie if it will get them the position, advantage, or goal they desire. They are arrogant, haughty, impudent, snooty, and insolent. They disdain, mock, slander, and speak ill of anyone who stands in the way of their ideology, and they freely use foul language. In this climate, parents will no longer be able to persuade, control, lead, or exercise authority over their own children. And although people were once thankful and appreciative, they will generally become void of gratitude and unappreciative of everything. Impurity will seep into society and cause it to become impure, ill-mannered, unclean, indecent, coarse, vulgar, offensive, crude, lewd, and rude.**
>
> **Love for and commitment to family will disintegrate, and divorce will become epidemic, with irreconcilable differences being a major factor in tearing families apart. In fact, every imaginable type of covenant will be regularly violated, and the court system will be overwhelmed as people go overboard, suing and being sued. People will generally lose the ability to**

say no and will be unable to control their instincts in nearly every area of life. People will become savage, and it will eventually feel like there are no laws to protect the innocent.

Friend, this sounds just like the days in which we are presently living, and the reason it does is, we're living at the very end of the age. God alerts us in these verses that when we see all these things and feel like we're surrounded by them on every side, we can know with certainty that we're in the last of the last days. Someone had to be the final generation, and it appears that the Holy Spirit has said to us, "TAG! You're it!"

But God didn't tell us these things to *scare* us — He told us to *prepare* us. He wants us to know what is coming so we'll get ready and strengthen ourselves spiritually. Through the empowerment of His Spirit, we can resist all these end-time temptations and live victoriously for Him.

The Holy Spirit Also Prophesied People Would Become...

As we continue our dissection of Paul's prophecy, we see that he went on to say that people would also become "traitors, heady, [and] highminded..." (2 Timothy 3:4). Written out in the original Greek, these words are:

Prodotai, propeteis, tetyphōmenoi...

As with all the previous words we have unpacked, these three also have a unique meaning. They are all plural in form, which means the presence of *traitorous*, *heady*, and *high-minded* people will not be an isolated case here and there. Instead, these types of individuals will be widespread throughout society.

There Will Be 'Traitors'

The word "traitors" found in Second Timothy 3:4 is the Greek word *prodotoi*, which is the plural form of *prodotes*, and it describes *one who is a traitor to an oath* or *one who betrays or abandons a friend*. It can also signify a lack of commitment to oaths or relationships or depict one who is treacherous in the context of an oath or a relationship. We could even translate this word as *a fair-weather friend*.

By using this word *prodotes*, the Holy Spirit is informing us that at the very end of the age, there will be a lackluster commitment to relationships. This condition will proliferate in society to such a degree that friendships will not be what they used to be.

With the world being made up of self-lovers, people will make themselves top priority. If they're faced with having to personally sacrifice something to keep their commitment to someone else, their response will tend toward breaking off the relationship that requires the commitment. Those who fit this description are often referred to as "fair-weather friends." As long as the "weather" is good in the relationship, he or she will be there. But if storms arise or the relationship is no longer convenient, that person's solution is to walk away. This tells us that the commitment — or oath — of friendship was on shaky ground from the beginning.

The word *prodotes* — translated here as "traitors" — depicts a *shallowness* of relationships that will develop between individuals at the end of the age. If you have experienced this type of fair-weather friends, you are not alone. Ask the Lord to heal your heart of all the hurt and disappointment. At the same time, learn the lesson of not treating others the way you were treated. Rather than cut ties and run when things get tough, pray for God's grace to dig in your heels and be a faithful friend, not a traitor.

'Heady' People Are Reckless and Impulsive

Besides traitors, the Bible says there will also be people who are "heady" (*see* 2 Timothy 3:4). This is a very poor translation of the Greek word *propetes*, which literally means *reckless* or *impulsive*. It can depict *people so wholly given to violence that they enjoy violence and become known for their violent, reckless, rash, emotional intemperance*. The Holy Spirit is using this word to tell us that in the last of the last days, many people will be given to violence and unable to control their tempers.

We've already seen in our previous lesson that violence and brutality make for the hottest-selling ticket today at the theater, on the Internet, in music, and in video games. People have developed a thirst for blood and violence in entertainment, and we are witnessing the long-term impact on society as acts of violence steadily increase in every area of modern culture. Random mass shootings in public places are an example of people being *reckless*, *violent*, and *impulsive* — what the Bible calls "heady."

If Jesus tarries and future historians look back on our time, what will they say about us? When we think of the Roman Empire and all the violence and bloodshed that went on in the Colosseum, we see their era as brutal. But what might people say about us when they look back and see the kind of movies we watched and video games we played in the name of "entertainment"? The mutilation and desecration of the human body — made in God's image to be His temple — is no small matter. It seriously grieves the heart of God. That said, here is something you really need to think about:

- If you took an honest look at your media cabinet or all your digital files of movies, television programs, songs, and so forth, how many of them do you think Jesus would be willing to watch or listen to with you? Would He sit down with you and say, "That's a good movie"?

- Maybe it's time for you to go through your files and do some housecleaning. Get rid of the things that you sense grieve and offend the Holy Spirit. Stop tolerating violent scenes and soul-desensitizing messages in your life and the lives of your loved ones. Any movie, TV program, video game, or music you believe Jesus would not sit and watch and listen to with you, you should strongly consider getting rid of — today!

Proverbs 4:23 says, "Keep thy heart with all diligence; for out of it are the issues of life." Friend, it is imperative that we set a guard over our hearts, minds, and emotions and not allow evil influences to enter us. We need to be careful about what goes into our eyes and into our ears. We will become what we behold.

The 'Highminded' Are Puffed Up With Pride

The next word the Holy Spirit adds in Second Timothy 3:4 to describe society at the end of the age is "highminded." This is a translation of the Greek word *tuphoo*, and it means *to be inflated with pride*. It pictures *one puffed up and clouded by his own sense of self-importance*. What's interesting is that this word is where we get the word *typhoon*, which brings us back to our introduction.

Think about what takes place when people are informed that a typhoon or hurricane is coming. They begin preparing for its arrival by picking up and putting away things that could be damaged or destroyed. Windows are boarded up; vehicles are driven to higher ground; and family and friends are taken out of harm's way.

The closer the storm gets, the darker the skies become and the more violently the winds rage. Everything looks ominous and foreboding. All of that is in this word "highminded" — the Greek word *tuphoo*.

By using this word, the Holy Spirit is telling us that at the end of days, there will be moments when it will look like society is rapidly degenerating right before our eyes into one huge mass of people who arrogantly deny God and are self-inflated with pride. It will almost seem like a typhoon or a hurricane when massive dark clouds, destructive winds, and heavy rain are moving in from the sea and over the landscape.

When a violent storm arrives, everything is affected *except for those who have taken appropriate shelter or who have fled from the storm*. And the good news is typhoons and hurricanes never last long! They are short-lived and eventually pass from the scene.

The Holy Spirit uses this word *tuphoo* to warn us that *stormy people* are coming — they are a prophesied part of the last of the last days. When we see them coming, we are to spiritually seek higher ground and batten down the hatches. Not only are we to find shelter to protect ourselves, but also to help protect others. We were born for such as time as this, and God has given us the answers that people need and that they are looking for.

Taking into account the original Greek meaning of the words we've studied, here is the *Renner Interpretive Version (RIV)* of Second Timothy 3:4 up to this point:

> **People will find it easy to walk away from commitments and to easily throw away relationships. They will become reckless, impulsive, and known for their enjoyment of violence. They will become full of pride and inflated with a sense of their own self-importance — to the extent that it may end up feeling like society is being hit by a typhoon; however, those menacing winds of change will eventually blow out like a storm that comes and goes....**

Friend, to effectively deal with those that are *traitorous*, *heady*, and *highminded*, we must arm ourselves with God's Word and the weapons of warfare He has provided (*see* Ephesians 6:14-18). Likewise, we must stay filled with the Holy Spirit and allow His power to flow through us so we can each run our race with endurance all the way to the end!

Questions and Answers With Rick Renner

In the program, Rick answered the following question from one of our viewers.

Q. How much should I pray in tongues?

A. To answer this question, we turn our attention to First Corinthians 14:18 where the apostle Paul said, "I thank my God, I speak with tongues more than ye all."

When he made this statement, he was speaking to the believers in Corinth who were known for speaking in tongues a great deal. Why did Paul put so much time and effort into speaking in tongues *more than all the Corinthians put together*? The answer is found in **First Corinthians 14:4**, which says:

He that speaketh in an unknown tongue *edifieth* himself....

Notice the word "edifieth." It is a form of the word *oikodomeo*, which is an architectural term used to describe a construction project in which walls were knocked out to make a room bigger. The use of this word here tells us that when you pray in tongues, you increase your spiritual capacity! Paul was literally saying that the more you pray in tongues, the more of the Holy Spirit's infilling you will receive.

So it is never possible to pray in tongues too much because every time you pray in tongues, you're expanding your spiritual capacity to receive more of the Spirit.

STUDY QUESTIONS

> **Study to shew thyself approved unto God, a workman that needeth not to be ashamed, rightly dividing the word of truth.**
> **— 2 Timothy 2:15**

1. Look up **Proverbs 4:23** in a few different Bible versions and *write out* the one that speaks to you most. In what ways can you better guard your eyes and ears — as well as that of your family — from the filth and violence proliferating in society? What ground rules can you establish to protect your hearts and minds from ungodly messages

and images? (Consider gathering your family to talk and pray about healthy solutions you can implement together.)

2. Someone who is "heady" is one who is *reckless*, *impulsive*, and even *violent* at times. Are you spending time with anyone like this? How about your children? What do First Corinthians 15:33 and Proverbs 13:20 and 22:24,25 say about the quality of the company you keep?

3. According to Ecclesiastes 4:9-12 and Proverbs 27:17, what value does true friendship bring into your life?

PRACTICAL APPLICATION

> **But be ye doers of the word, and not hearers only, deceiving your own selves.**
> **—James 1:22**

1. Who are you blessed with in your life that you consider a true, genuine friend? What is it about them that energizes you with life and strength and causes you to appreciate them so much? Have you told them lately that you are thankful for them being your friend? How can you express your love and appreciation to them in a way that will truly bless them?

2. If we could interview the people you're in a relationship with, would they describe you as a *fair-weather friend* or a *true friend*? What evidence might they offer to support their answer? What adjustments can you make to come up higher and be a better friend to those with whom you're in relationship?

3. Have you been hurt by a fair-weather friend? Did they abandon you when you needed them most? Jesus knows how you feel…in His hour of greatest need, His 12 closest companions abandoned Him. Take a few moments to pray and ask the Holy Spirit to bring healing to your heart. If you're holding unforgiveness toward this person, ask God to forgive you and release them into God's hands (*see* Mark 11:25). By faith, pray a blessing over them and you will be blessed in return (*see* 1 Peter 3:8,9).

LESSON 11

TOPIC
Pandemics, Hedonism, and Spiritual Mannequins

SCRIPTURES
1. **2 Timothy 3:1** — This know also, that in the last days perilous times shall come.
2. **2 Timothy 3:4,5** — Traitors, heady, highminded, lovers of pleasures more than lovers of God; having a form of godliness, but denying the power thereof: from such turn away.

GREEK WORDS
1. "lovers of pleasures" — **φιλήδονος** (*philedonos*): from **φίλος** (*philos*) and **ἡδονή** (*hedone*); the word **φίλος** (*philos*) means love; the word **ἡδονή** (*hedone*) means pleasure; the root of the word hedonism; denotes individuals who give themselves to the unbridled and unrestrained seeking of pleasures of any type; to love pleasure; to live for the fulfillment of one's pleasure
2. "more than" — **μᾶλλον** (*mallon*): more than; more than what it is compared to; in comparison to; it involves rank as compared to something else; the higher and more important priority over the less important
3. "form" — **μόρφωσις** (*morphosis*): an outward shape or form; it speaks only of an outward shape and nothing of content
4. "godliness" — **εὐσέβεια** (*eusebeia*): piety or religiosity; includes actions, clerical clothing, religious styles, religious words, religious phrases, religious symbols, and other external religious trappings that people associate with someone or something that is religious
5. "denying" — **ἀρνέομαι** (*arneomai*): to deny, disown, reject, refuse, or renounce
6. "turn away" — **ἀποτρέπω** (*apotrepo*): from **ἀπό** (*apo*) and **τροπή** (*trope*); the word **ἀπό** (*apo*) means away; the word **τροπή** (*trope*)

means to turn; compounded, it means to turn away from; depicts either a mental, spiritual, or physical turning

SYNOPSIS

According to Jesus, the greatest thing you can do is "…love the Lord your God with all your heart, and with all your soul, and with all your strength, and with all your mind…" (Luke 10:27 *TLB*). Outward appearances and going through the motions are a waste of time. As King David said, "… A flawless performance is nothing to you…" (Psalm 51:16 *MSG*). Sincere love and devotion straight from your heart is what pleases God.

In this day and age, when being "spiritual mannequins" is the new normal, we need to be reminded that it's what's inside us that really counts. It's time we get back to the basics — we must return to believing in the truth of the Bible and the power of the Blood of Christ, praying in the mighty name of Jesus and cooperating with and trusting in the transforming power of the Holy Spirit. Practices like these will protect us from the last-days masquerade that is playing out on the societal scene worldwide.

The emphasis of this lesson:

The Holy Spirit prophesied that in the last days, people will be lovers of pleasure more than lovers of God and that there will even be individuals in the Church who have a form of godliness but deny and refute the transforming power of God.

A Review of Our Anchor Verse

To help us keep the foundation of this end-times series in focus, let's look again at Paul's opening words in Second Timothy 3:1, where he said, "This know also, that in the last days perilous times shall come." Taking the original Greek of this verse into account, here is the *Renner Interpretive Version* (*RIV*) of Second Timothy 3:1:

> **You emphatically and categorically need to know with unquestionable certainty that in the very end of days — when time has sailed to its last port and no more time remains for the journey — that last season will stand in the midst of uncontrollable, unpredictable, hurtful, treacherous, and menacing times that will be emotionally difficult for people to bear.**

This is a clear description of the very times in which we are living. Unpredictable, uncontrollable, and menacing situations are standing up all around us. Yet we have the same Spirit that raised Jesus from the dead living inside us! We have been appointed and anointed by God to live in this period, and with His strength, we can march victoriously all the way to the end.

What Is Meant by the Words 'Traitors,' 'Heady,' and 'Highminded'?

In our last lesson, we examined Paul's prophetic vision of the last days in Second Timothy 3:4, where he informed us that people will also become "traitors, heady, [and] highminded…." As we've noted, these three words are all in plural form, which means the presence of *traitorous*, *heady*, and *high-minded* people will be widespread throughout society — not an isolated incident.

In the original Greek, this part of the verse reads:

Prodotai, propeteis, tetuphomenoi…

"Traitors" is the Greek word *prodotai*, and it basically describes *fair-weather friends*. If the "weather" in a relationship is good, people remain together. But if a "storm" of disagreement kicks up — or if staying committed to the relationship is inconvenient — one or both parties will choose to part ways. Thus, at the very end of the age, friendship will not be what it once was.

"Heady" is the Greek word *propeteis*, a word describing those who are *reckless*, *impulsive*, and *violent*. The Holy Spirit is using this word to tell us that at the very end of the age, many people will be given to violence and unable to control their tempers. The steady increase in mass shootings is a manifestation of this word *propeteis*.

"Highminded" is the word *tetuphomenoi*, which is from the word *tuphos*, a word that depicts *one puffed up and clouded by his own sense of self-importance*. It is where we get the term "typhoon." The Holy Spirit uses this word to tell us that at the end of the age, the attitude and behavior of some people will feel like a typhoon or hurricane has blown in.

When things look dark, ominous, and overwhelming, we are to spiritually batten down the hatches and seek the protection of God — for ourselves and those we love. The good news is that just as hurricanes and typhoons blow in, they also blow out, and when they are over, we are to use the wisdom and guidance of the Holy Spirit to help rebuild. Although the devil will try to bring about disaster, we are the Church of the Lord Jesus Christ, and the gates of hell shall not prevail against us (*see* Matthew 16:18)!

Taking into account the original Greek meaning of these words, here is the *Renner Interpretive Version* (*RIV*) of the latter part of Second Timothy 3:4:

> **People will find it easy to walk away from commitments and to easily throw away relationships. They will become reckless, impulsive, and known for their enjoyment of violence. They will become full of pride and inflated with a sense of their own self-importance — to the extent that it may end up feeling like society is being hit by a typhoon; however, those menacing winds of change will eventually blow out like a storm that comes and goes....**

Aren't you grateful that the evil in the last days will not rein forever? It will blow in, and God will blow it out.

People Will Be 'Lovers of Pleasure'

The Bible says that in addition to being traitorous, heady, and high-minded, people at the end of the age will also be "...lovers of pleasures more than lovers of God" (2 Timothy 3:4). Notice the phrase "lovers of pleasures." It is the Greek word *philedonoi*, the plural form of *philedonos*, which is a compound of the words *philos* and *hedone*. The word *philos* means *love*, and the word *hedone* means *pleasure* and is the root of the English word "hedonism," which denotes *those who give themselves to the unbridled and unrestrained seeking of pleasures of any type*.

When these two words *philos* and *hedone* are joined to form the new word *philedonos* — translated in Second Timothy 3:4 as "lovers of pleasure" — it means *to love pleasure* or *to live for the fulfillment of one's pleasure*. This is a picture of people who are completely preoccupied with their own self-gratification or of those who have made personal happiness their highest aspiration in life. The use of this word tells us that at the end of the age, people will be obsessed with a non-stop pursuit of pleasure and happiness.

Although there is nothing wrong with being happy, it should never be our primary pursuit. Happiness is based on *what's happening*, and any good feelings resulting from present circumstances will always come and go. Pursuing happiness is like running on a treadmill — you will be running for a long, long time, without actually moving forward, and you will wear yourself out.

Instead of pursuing happiness, which is temporary, we need to pursue *obedience to God*. When we obey God, we have *joy*, and joy supersedes happiness, providing supernatural strength that can't be found any other place.

Paul qualifies the extent of this pleasure-craving crowd by saying they will be "…lovers of pleasure *more than* lovers of God" (2 Timothy 3:4). The words "more than" are a translation of the Greek word *mallon*, which means *more than*, but specifically *more than what it is compared to*. It can also be translated *in comparison to*, as it involves rank as compared to something else. It indicates *the higher and more important priority over the less important*.

In this passage, the comparison deals with people being lovers of pleasure "more than" (*mallon*) lovers of God. The word "lovers" is again the word *philos*, meaning *to love* or *have affection for*, and the word for "God" is *Theos*. Notice it doesn't say they will *not* love God — rather, it says their love and affection for Him will be *much less in comparison* to their love and pursuit of self-gratification and pleasure.

This will be a major sign that we have reached the very end of the age — people in society will be constantly seeking another thrill or pleasure to make them happy. And their pursuit of pleasure will supersede their affection and pursuit of God.

Many Will Have a 'Form of Godliness'

In Second Timothy 3:5, the Bible says the last-days society will include those "having a form of godliness, but denying the power thereof…." There are several important words in this passage, including the word "having," which is a form of the Greek word *echo*, meaning *to have, to hold*, or *to possess*. The word "form" is the Greek word *morphosis*, and it describes *an outward shape or form*. It speaks only of an outward shape and nothing of content. So when Paul prophesied that people would "have a form" of godliness, he was saying that many in the last days — including a portion of the Church — would have all the right words and appearances in their religious practices, but would lack the *power* of God because they would "deny" its operation.

One of the best ways to explain this is by using the example of a *mannequin*. Today, mannequins nearly look human. To a casual onlooker, many mannequins, because they are so lifelike, could pass for a real human. You could bump into one in the store and apologize, mistaking it for an actual person.

This example of a mannequin vividly depicts how people in the last of the last days will be so developed outwardly with the right godly form, but they're nothing more than a shell — on the inside they're empty. Here, the Holy Spirit is foretelling that some religious groups at the end of the age will externally have a "form" of godliness, but they will lack the inner power that makes godliness real. They will look and sound good, but at the end of the day, they will be devoid of spiritual power and will lack spiritual effectiveness.

This brings us to the word "godliness," which is a translation of the Greek word *eusebeia*, and in this verse, it denotes *piety* or *religiosity*. This "outer form" used to depict godliness could include clerical clothing, religious styles, religious words, religious actions, religious phrases, religious symbols, and other external religious trappings that people associate with someone or something that is *religious* or even *spiritual*.

In the context of Second Timothy 3:5, the Holy Spirit is saying that there will be people at the end of the age who possess all the right external paraphernalia of godliness — the right words, symbols, and actions. They may even wear religious clothing or have a cross draped around their necks and a Bible in their hands. Some may even have a strong social-media presence with pious-sounding posts. But these people will be like "spiritual mannequins" dressed up in religious clothing — having the right outward "form of godliness" but lacking the inward, life-giving power of God.

Just imagine a mannequin dressed like a minister of the Gospel positioned in front of you. It's wearing clerical clothing, including a gold-chained cross draped across its chest and posed with a big Bible in its hands. Outwardly it looks like the real deal, but the fact is, it's just a mannequin. It is merely a shell devoid of all life.

This is what the Holy Spirit, through Paul, prophesied would take place at the end of the age. There will be people who have the right *outward* form of godliness, but they will be *inwardly* empty. Although this won't be everyone in the Church, it will be a significant number. They'll look and play the part of a Christian, but like a mannequin, they'll be empty shells who are devoid of God's power.

They Will 'Deny the Power' of God

Paul went on to say these "spiritual mannequins" would be guilty of "denying the power thereof" (*see* 2 Timothy 3:5). The word "denying" here is the Greek word *arneomai*, which means *to deny, disown, reject, refuse,* or *renounce*. As unbelievable as it sounds, a time is coming — and is *already here* — when some spiritual leaders will reject and renounce the genuine operation of God's power. When confronted with the true power of the Gospel that can transform lives, these apostate leaders will reject God's truth and embrace a lie.

History reveals that many traditional denominational churches were born in revival and in the power of the Holy Spirit. They were pioneered by men and women who believed the Bible and gave their lives for the preaching of the Gospel. But sadly, not all traditional churches have stayed loyal to their original, God-given message and mission.

In order to meet new societal norms, these denominations have gradually compromised the truth and moved in the direction of modifying the Gospel wherever needed to avoid controversy or to better "fit in." As a result, a watered-down Gospel is being presented in these "last of the last days" that marginalizes sin and does not recognize the need to repent. Instead, those who propagate this false Gospel suggest that the real problem with human beings is psychological or medical and can be treated by acceptance, inclusion, proper conditioning, medication, or even a surgical procedure.

This trend to throw open the doors to every possible lifestyle — regardless of how unscriptural — under the banner of God's love and tolerance is creeping into historical denominational churches across the world. Truly we are living in an end-time society when "spiritual mannequins" have become the order of the day in large segments of the Church.

How Does God Say We Are To Respond to This?

In Second Timothy 3:5, the apostle Paul said we are to "turn away" from such people and such churches. The words "turn away" are a translation of the Greek word *apotrepo*, which is from the words *apo* and *trope*. The word *apo* means *away*, and the word *trope* means *to turn*. When compounded, the word *apotrepo* means *to turn away from* and depicts either *a mental*, *spiritual*, or *physical turning*.

The Greek tense in this verse is so strong that it cannot be misunderstood. Through Paul, the Holy Spirit is commanding all believers — including *us* — to withdraw from spiritual mannequins — those who have a form of godliness but deny, disown, reject, and renounce God's power. This *turning away* carries the idea of putting distance between yourself and this compromised and corrupted atmosphere immediately. Initially, this turning away is *spiritual* and *mental*, but because there is a physical component to this word, we can know that, if need be, we must also *physically turn away* and *remove ourselves* from that apostate environment.

Taking into account the original Greek meaning of these words, here is the *Renner Interpretive Version* (*RIV*) of Second Timothy 3:5:

> **Although they may possess an outward form of religiosity, they will rebuff, refute, refuse, and reject the authentic power that goes along with genuine godliness. I urgently tell you to mentally, spiritually, and physically turn away from and remove yourselves from such people.**

Friend, none of us is immune to becoming a mere "form of godliness." Even the most anointed and sincere and devoted believers can gradually become spiritual mannequins over time. So continue to stoke the fire of passion and desire for Jesus! Keep pulling away daily to spend time in His presence and in His Word. Invite the Holy Spirit to breathe new life into your spirit every day, and you will truly thrive in this end-time age!

Questions and Answers With Rick Renner

In the program, Rick answered the following question from one of our viewers.

Q. Did Jesus ever talk about UFOs?

A. In this day and age when disclosure on the subject of unidentified aerial phenomena — also known as UFOs — continues to increase, many people wonder if Jesus ever talked about it. What's interesting is that Jesus *possibly* alludes to UFOs in Luke 21:11. In this passage, where He is talking about the signs we would see before His return and the end of the age, He says:

> **And great earthquakes shall be in divers places, and famines, and pestilences; and fearful sights** *and great signs shall there be from heaven.*

Clearly, Jesus is saying that at the end of the age, there will be fearful sights and great signs "from heaven" (Luke 21:11). The word "from" in this verse is the Greek word *apo*, which is a preposition meaning *from* or *directly from*. Thus, fearful sights and great signs will descend *directly from heaven*, or from *the heavens*.

So while Jesus didn't explicitly say these would be UFOs, He did say at the very end of the age there would be things appearing and descending *directly out of the heavens*. What are those "fearful sights"? We'll take a closer look in our next lesson.

STUDY QUESTIONS

> **Study to shew thyself approved unto God, a workman that needeth not to be ashamed, rightly dividing the word of truth.**
> **— 2 Timothy 2:15**

1. According to First John 4:19, John 3:16, and Romans 5:6-8, why should you live your life to love and please God? (Also consider Ephesians 2:4-9.)
2. Another important — and sobering — reason for living to please God is found in Second Corinthians 5:9 and 10 (as well as Hebrews 9:27; Romans 14:10-12, and Revelation 22:12). Read these passages and identify this powerful motivating factor. How do these verses stir your faith and encourage you to live according to godly standards?
3. Scripture is filled with examples of individuals and nations that started their relationship with God fully ablaze, but over time they gradually fizzled out. What person or nation in the Bible comes to mind that experienced this? Why do you think their example stands out to you?

4. When God gave us the Ten Commandments through Moses, He voiced His desire to be *first* and to be our One and only Love. Carefully read Exodus 20:1-4 — as if God Himself is standing in front of and speaking directly to you. What is He speaking to you personally through this passage? (Also consider Isaiah 42:8; 1 John 5:21; Matthew 22:36-38.)

PRACTICAL APPLICATION

> **But be ye doers of the word, and not hearers only, deceiving your own selves.**
> **—James 1:22**

1. What would you say is the *driving force* of your life: love for God or personal happiness? Which is greater: your desire to please Him in all you do, or self-gratification? To help you answer accurately, take a look at your calendar and your checkbook. Where is most of your time and money being spent? This is a real-life indicator of what is truly motivating your life.

2. Although most people today are not bowing down to an idol made of stone as they did in the past, many have modified the truth of God's Word to accommodate their lifestyles, thus creating their own "image" of who God is. How about you? Are there some parts of Scripture you hold onto but other parts you ignore? Have you created your own *image* of who God is? What is the Holy Spirit showing you about yourself through this lesson?

3. Have you become a Christian in name only? Are you just going through the religious motions — talking the talk and looking the part — or are you really loving and serving God with all your heart, all your soul, all your mind, and all your strength?

4. Take a few moments to pray as David prayed: "Search me, O God, and know my heart; test my thoughts. Point out anything you find in me that makes you sad, and lead me along the path of everlasting life" (Psalm 139:23,24 *TLB*). Listen for what the Holy Spirit speaks to you. If He shows you any areas where you need improvement, repent and surrender those things to Him, taking any action steps He reveals.

LESSON 12

TOPIC
Creeps!

SCRIPTURES
1. **2 Timothy 3:1** — This know also, that in the last days perilous times shall come.
2. **2 Timothy 3:4-6** — Traitors, heady, highminded, lovers of pleasures more than lovers of God; having a form of godliness, but denying the power thereof: from such turn away. For of this sort are they which creep into houses, and lead captive silly women laden with sins, led away with divers lusts.

GREEK WORDS
1. "turn away" — ἀποτρέπω (*apotrepo*): from ἀπό (*apo*) and τροπή (*trope*); the word ἀπό (*apo*) means away; the word τροπή (*trope*) means to turn; compounded, it means to turn away from; depicts either a mental, spiritual, or physical turning
2. "creep into" — ἐνδύνω (*enduno*): to be clothed; to hide in; to be clothed with; to disguise by wrapping oneself in a garment; to creep into; to find access
3. "houses" — οἰκία (*oikia*): households; homes; residences; families
4. "lead captive" — αἰχμαλωτίζω (*aichmalotidzo*): to take captive at a spear point; to take captive as a prisoner; to put the spear into the back of a captive and forcibly drive him into captivity; manipulation by physical force or by mental or spiritual suggestion
5. "silly women" — γυναικάριον (*gunaikarion*): needy women; weak women; women who feel a sense of need

SYNOPSIS
No one's birth is random or accidental — including yours. The Bible says every day of your life was written in God's book before one of them took place (*see* Psalm 139:16), and He has purposely appointed you to live in this period of history (*see* Acts 17:26). You've been tagged by the Holy

Spirit to live at the very end of the age, and what is truly mindboggling is that you're living in the fulfillment of what was spoken by the prophets thousands of years ago.

Since God called you and chose you to live now, He has also anointed you to help bring Heaven to earth and bring the lost of earth to Heaven. He gave us Second Timothy 3 to alert us and awaken us to what's happening in the world so that we don't become victims of the evil that is taking place.

Think of the people that you know who are suffering in some area of their lives because of the nonsense going on in society. The systems of the world are collapsing and people are spiraling out of control, but God has given you the answers they need! Therefore, "You are to live clean, innocent lives as children of God in a dark world full of people who are crooked and stubborn. Shine out among them like beacon lights, holding out to them the Word of Life…" (Philippians 2:15,16 *TLB*).

The emphasis of this lesson:

The Holy Spirit prophesied through Paul that in the last days, the enemy would stealthily find access into people's homes to manipulate the needy and take captive those who are burdened and overwhelmed with personal failures, problems, and disappointments in life.

The *Renner Interpretive Version* (*RIV*) of Our Anchor Verse

Nearly 2,000 years ago, the Spirit of God moved on the apostle Paul and prophesied saying, "This know also, that in the last days perilous times shall come" (2 Timothy 3:1). Here is a review of the *Renner Interpretive Version* (*RIV*) of this foundational verse:

> You emphatically and categorically need to know with unquestionable certainty that in the very end of days — when time has sailed to its last port and no more time remains for the journey — that last season will stand in the midst of uncontrollable, unpredictable, hurtful, treacherous, and menacing times that will be emotionally difficult for people to bear.

After alerting us of the fact that unprecedented, turbulent times would prevail in the last of the last days, Paul began to describe more than two dozen characteristics of society that would take place. We have covered many of these menacing conditions in our previous lessons, including the fact that people will be "traitors, heady, highminded, lovers of pleasures more than lovers of God" (2 Timothy 3:4).

In this lesson, we will pull back the curtain to learn what Paul meant when he told us about people who "creep into houses and lead captive silly women" (*see* 2 Timothy 3:6).

But first, let's recap what Paul prophesied in Second Timothy 3:5.

'Spiritual Mannequins' Will Be the Order of the Day at the End of the Age

Paul said that at the end of the age, in addition to seeing people with an obsession for pleasure and self-gratification, we would see individuals, "having a form of godliness, but denying the power thereof…" (2 Timothy 3:5). We learned that the word "form" is the Greek word *morphosis*, which describes *an outward shape or form that lacks inward substance.*

We also saw that the word "godliness" is the Greek word *eusebeia*, which speaks of *piety* or *religiosity*, and it includes not only *clerical clothing*, but also *religious styles, religious words, religious phrases, religious symbols, religious actions, and other external religious trappings that people associate with someone or something that is religious or spiritual.* When we take the meanings of the words "form" and "godliness" and put them together, the phrase "having a form of godliness" can best be described as a *spiritual mannequin.*

Essentially, Paul prophesied that at the very end of the age, spiritual mannequins would emerge in the Church. These could be individuals who dress like a minister of the Gospel, wearing the *religious paraphernalia* and playing the part of a Christian. But like mannequins, they are *empty shells*, lacking the inner substance of God and devoid of all life. Hence, a spiritual mannequin is one who looks like a believer on the outside in what he wears, what he says, and how he acts. He may even have a cross around his neck and a Bible in his hands, but on the inside he is empty.

Paul added that while these people would look the part on the outside, they would live "…denying the power thereof…" (2 Timothy 3:5). The word "denying" is the Greek word *arneomai*, which means *to deny, disown, reject, refuse,* or *renounce.* The use of this word tells us that in the very last days, spiritual leaders will arise in the Church who *reject* and *disown* the authentic operation of God's power and God's Word and, instead, embrace a lie.

In order to avoid controversy, adapt to the new cultural norms of society, and better "fit in," these leaders will modify the Gospel wherever they deem needed. This trend of throwing open the doors to every possible lifestyle, no matter how unscriptural, under the banner of God's love and tolerance is creeping into historical denominational churches across the world. As a result, a watered-down Gospel is being presented in these last days that marginalizes sin, doesn't recognize the need to repent, and suggests that the real problem with human beings is psychological or medical and can be treated by acceptance, inclusion, proper conditioning, and even medication or surgery. This is a picture of *an apostate Church*.

Paul said clearly, "…From such turn away" (2 Timothy 3:5). The phrase "turn away" is the Greek word *apotrepo*, which is from the word *apo*, meaning *away*, and the word *trope*, meaning *to turn*. When compounded, they form the word *apotrepo*, which means *to turn away from*, and it depicts either *a mental*, *spiritual*, or *physical turning away*. Basically, Paul said, "If you're part of an apostate group that's drifting away from the truth of God's Word, don't stick around with the hope of turning things around. Detach from them *mentally*, *spiritually*, and *physically* — put space between you and them and then pray for them from a distance."

When we insert the Greek meaning of all these words, the *Renner Interpretive Version* (*RIV*) of Second Timothy 3:5 reads:

Though they may possess an outward form of religiosity, they will rebuff, refute, refuse, and reject the authentic power that goes along with genuine godliness; you must mentally, spiritually, and physically turn away from such people.

The Greek word *apotrepo* — translated here as "turn away" — is very strong, which means this is not a suggestion but a *command*. If you remain in close relationship with a group that is drifting, you're in danger of drifting with them. That's why the Holy Spirit is commanding all of us to withdraw from spiritual mannequins — those who have a form of godliness but deny, disown, reject, and renounce God's power.

What Does 'Creep Into Houses' Mean?

Paul went on to describe how these spiritual mannequins would act, saying, "For of this sort are they which creep into houses, and lead captive silly women laden with sins, led away with divers lusts" (2 Timothy 3:6). Upon your first reading of this verse, it may seem very strange. But as we examine the meaning of some of its key words, it will become clearer.

First, notice the phrase "of this sort." In Greek, it is *ek touton*; the word *ek* means *out*, and the word *touton* means *of this group* or *out of this group*. The "group" being referred to is the group of apostate believers who are drifting away and distancing themselves from the authority of God's Word. They have a form of godliness but have diluted and modified the truth of Scripture to be inclusive and tolerant of people who are living ungodly lifestyles.

It is this very group of apostates that God said will "creep into houses" (*see* 2 Timothy 3:6). This phrase is a translation of the Greek words *hoi endunontes*, which is the plural form of the word *enduno*, and it means *to be clothed*, *to hide in*, or *to be clothed with*. In this case, it means *to disguise by wrapping oneself in a garment*. Thus, the "creeps" God wants us to be aware of are the "spiritual mannequins" who dress in a disguise to make themselves — and their message — more appealing in order to gain access into people's lives.

To be clear, this word *enduno* describes *a stealth operation* by which these "pretend believers" creep into and find access into "houses." In Greek, the word "houses" is *oikias*, which describes *households*, *homes*, *residences*, or *families*. Again, this depicts a clandestine or undercover operation to gain access into people's private spaces. It's interesting to note that the word "into" is a form of the Greek word *eis*, which means *into* and carries the idea of *penetration*. Hence, these make-believe ministers are stealthily trying to make a *penetration* into households, homes, or residences.

In the past, when people saw the phrase "creep into houses," many wondered, *Who are these people that are creeping into others' houses?* But now we understand. From the vantage point of our present, high-tech age, we see that the Holy Spirit was likely referring to the age of technology when radio, television, cable systems, and the Internet create an environment that makes "creeping into houses" very easy.

For example, at the time of this writing, there are more than 4.48 billion active Internet users in the world. Even those living in the most remote places on the planet can tap into a seemingly limitless source of information and media through all kinds of devices, including computers, tablets, and cell phones. Again, the "creeps" that are trying to worm their way into people's homes are those who have abandoned the Gospel and modified its message to fit in and be accepted by society.

Are you beginning to see why it is so important to be mindful of who and what you're watching and listening to online and on television? You need to know who these influencers really are, what they believe, and if they practice what they preach in their private lives. The Bible says, "…Don't believe everything you hear. Carefully weigh and examine what people tell you. Not everyone who talks about God comes from God. There are a lot of lying preachers loose in the world" (1 John 4:1 *MSG*). Friend, your eyes and ears are entryways into your mind and heart, and you need to guard them diligently — for you and for your family.

Who Are 'Silly Women Laden With Sins'?

Paul tells us that the goal of these apostate believers is to "…lead captive silly women…" (2 Timothy 3:6). The words "lead captive" is a very strange Greek word, which means *to take captive at a spear point; to take captive as a prisoner*. It is an ancient Greek word that depicts *putting the point of a spear into the back of a captive and forcibly driving him into captivity*. Thus, it came to denote the idea of *manipulation by physical force or by mental or spiritual suggestion*.

By using this word, the Holy Spirit prophesied that a time would come when the devil would begin to manipulate people with information that creeps into their homes under the disguise of "help." And according to Second Timothy 3:6, the primary target of this erroneous help is "silly women," which is a poor translation.

In Greek, the phrase "silly women" is the word *gunaikarion*, and it describes *needy women* or *weak women*. It doesn't have anything to do with women being foolish or ignorant. It really refers to women — or possibly men — who are living in the last of the last days and who feel an acute sense of need in their lives.

Specifically, the Scripture says these people are "laden with sins" (*see* 2 Timothy 3:6). The word "laden" is the Greek word *soreuo*, which means *to feel burdened, loaded,* or *overwhelmed*, and the Greek word for "sins" is *hamartia*, which means *to miss the mark of what was hoped for*. In this particular verse, it describes *personal failures, problems,* or *those who have experienced disappointments in life*.

Thus, the phrase "silly women laden with sins" is a picture of a needy person who is burdened or overwhelmed with personal failures, problems, or disappointments. Considering the technology of our time and the ease of access to the Internet, we can picture these people in their weakened condition, sitting in the privacy of their homes as they surf and scroll on their phones or computer, looking for answers to ease their hurting soul. Before long, something begins to resonate with and appeal to their sense of failure or disappointment, and it takes them captive.

Unmet Longings Can Become an Open Door to Evil Influencers

Paul said that this particular type of person would be "…led away with divers lusts" (2 Timothy 3:6). The word "lusts" is a form of the Greek word *epithumia*, and it describes *one's deepest longings*. The use of all these Greek words together indicates that many weak, needy people will be desperate to find help at the very end of the age.

Often smooth-talking worldly voices in the disguise of "help" will appear and tug on people's hearts to manipulate their emotions and lead them in a wrong direction. This passage paints a picture of a person in a weakened, vulnerable condition in the privacy of his or her home who is sincerely and desperately searching for answers to alleviate his or her pain and inner struggles. Then, suddenly, someone "creeps into the house" through some form of media and appears to address the person's needs.

Statistics show that the primary audience across most platforms of media is women, which is why advertisers and business owners spend the bulk of their dollars trying to reach women. They are the primary target because if women can be convinced that a product is needed, that house is going to buy that product. Satan understands this principle, which is why he targeted Eve in the Garden of Eden and why he will target women in their homes at the end of the age. If the devil can take the woman of the house captive, he can eventually gain control of the home.

Therefore, he relentlessly makes his appeal to those who are frustrated with their lives and overwhelmed with disappointments concerning their marriage, their finances, and their dreams — all the while trying to draw them into his "web" of deception.

Putting the meanings of all these words together, here is the *Renner Interpretive Version* (*RIV*) of Second Timothy 3:6:

> These sorts of people project themselves as "help" with the intention of gaining access into people's homes to manipulate them — especially women who feel overwhelmed by frustrations and disappointing failures in life, whom the manipulators find easier to influence because those people have so many unmet longings.

Questions and Answers With Rick Renner

In the program, Rick answered the following question from one of our viewers.

Q. What does the Bible say about monsters?

A. It may surprise you to know that Jesus Himself said something about monsters in Luke 21:11. As we noted in the last lesson, Jesus is talking in this passage about the signs we would see before His return and at the end of the age. Specifically, He said:

> And great earthquakes shall be in divers places, and famines, and pestilences; and fearful sights and great signs shall there be from heaven.

Notice the words "fearful sights." They are a translation of the Greek word *phobetron*, which is precisely the ancient Greek word for *monsters*. There is no question about it. It is a derivative of the word *phobos*, the term for *a fear*. But when the word *phobos* becomes *phobetron*, it describes *monsters* or *something monstrous*.

Hence, it seems that in Luke 21:11, Jesus is saying that at the end of the age, there will be *monsters* —or *something monstrous* — that shall descend "from heaven" (Luke 21:11). Remember, we learned that the word "from" in this verse is the Greek word *apo*, which is a preposition meaning *from*, or *directly from*. Thus, *monsters* or *monstrous things* will descend *directly from the heavens*.

STUDY QUESTIONS

> Study to shew thyself approved unto God, a workman that
> needeth not to be ashamed, rightly dividing the word of truth.
> — 2 Timothy 2:15

1. All of us go through times when we are confronted with personal failures, problems, or disappointments. Where is the first place you normally turn when you find yourself in such a situation? How effective and rewarding has this been for you?
2. Jesus talked at length about the *anxieties* and *worries* of life in Matthew 6:25-34. Take some time to reflect on His words as well as the wisdom of Philippians 4:6-8. What is the Holy Spirit showing you in these passages? According to these truths, how are you to respond when you're hit and overcome by worry and anxiety?
3. Do you need answers for your life? Do you want to know why you're acting the way you're acting and feeling the way you're feeling about things? Meditate on God's powerful promise to you in James 1:5 and take time now to put it into practice and receive the wisdom you need. (Also consider Proverbs 2:3-7.)

PRACTICAL APPLICATION

> But be ye doers of the word, and not hearers only,
> deceiving your own selves.
> — James 1:22

1. The Holy Spirit told us that one of the characteristics we would see in the last days is the enemy would begin to stealthily bring evil right into the privacy of our homes (*see* 2 Timothy 3:6). Have you experienced this? If so, in what ways?
2. When you hear that an estimated 4.48 billion people are active Internet users and have instant access to a seemingly limitless supply of information and media options, what does that say to you?
3. Satan is well aware of the struggles we experience, and therefore he relentlessly makes his appeal to us when we're frustrated with our lives and overwhelmed with disappointments. How has the enemy used "the web" in your life to try to take you captive in his lies? What device(s) has he attempted to use again and again? What pattern can you see in his efforts? Pray and ask the Holy Spirit for a specific plan of action to

keep you from falling in these areas (*see* 1 Corinthians 10:13; Isaiah 30:21; 42:16).

4. Is it any wonder God said, "Lest Satan should take advantage of us; for we are not [to be] ignorant of his *devices*" (2 Corinthians 2:11 *NKJV*). What practical boundaries might you set up to protect yourself and your family members from being taken captive by today's latest *devices*?

LESSON 13

TOPIC

Reprobates!

SCRIPTURES

1. **2 Timothy 3:1** — This know also, that in the last days perilous times shall come.
2. **2 Timothy 3:4-8** — Traitors, heady, highminded, lovers of pleasures more than lovers of God; having a form of godliness, but denying the power thereof: from such turn away. For of this sort are they which creep into houses, and lead captive silly women laden with sins, led away with divers lusts, ever learning, and never able to come to the knowledge of the truth. Now as Jannes and Jambres withstood Moses, so do these also resist the truth: men of corrupt minds, reprobate concerning the faith.

GREEK WORDS

1. "withstood" — ἀνθίστημι (*anthistemi*): to stand against; to stand in opposition; it demonstrates the attitude of one who is fiercely opposed to something and therefore determines to do everything within his power to resist it; to stand against it; to withstand; to defy
2. "resist" — ἀνθίστημι (*anthistemi*): to stand against; to stand in opposition; it demonstrates the attitude of one who is fiercely opposed to something and therefore determines to do everything within his power to resist it; to stand against it; to withstand; to defy
3. "corrupt" — **καταφθείρω** (*kataphtheiro*): from **κατά** (*kata*) and φθείρω (*phtheiro*); the word **κατά** (*kata*) means down; the word

φθείρω (*phtheiro*) means corruption, degeneration, or deterioration; hence, to move downward into a state of collapse, deterioration, and ruin; only used in 2 Timothy 3:8
4. "minds" — νοῦς (*nous*): plural, minds; the ability to think, reason, understand, or to comprehend; the place from which one rules and controls his inward and outward environment; the central control center for a human being; the place where reasoning, perception, and understanding take place
5. "reprobate" — ἀδόκιμος (*adokimos*): unfit; rejected; anything rejected due to its flawed nature; depicts a mind that has become unfit and defective; the mind of an individual or the mind of society that has become ill-affected, especially in regard to conclusions about moral issues; a reprobate mind eventually produces reprobate behaviors; defective; malfunctioning
6. "the faith" — τὴν πίστιν (*ten pistin*): with a definite article, "the" faith; "the" doctrine; "the" non-negotiable tenants of the Christian faith

SYNOPSIS

In addition to the "creeps" who stealthily slither their way into people's homes to manipulate the weak and the needy, there is another major sign we need to be on the lookout for — but this one will specifically affect the Church. The apostle Paul said, "Now as Jannes and Jambres withstood Moses, so do these also resist the truth: men of corrupt minds, reprobate concerning the faith" (2 Timothy 3:8). Who were Jannes and Jambres, what do they have to do with the last days, and what does it mean to be "reprobate concerning the faith"? The Holy Spirit through Paul had a lot to say about this subject and He emphatically warned against allowing this type of influence in your life.

The emphasis of this lesson:

In the last days, an apostate Church will emerge in which men of corrupt minds will spread reprobate thinking concerning the timeless truth of Scripture. Eventually, their spiritual nonsense will become clear to all men, but that won't stop them from deceiving and being deceived.

A Quick Review of Second Timothy 3:1,4-6

Before we dive in and begin examining Second Timothy 3:8, let's take a few moments to reflect on our foundational verse and the verses we've been studying in the last few lessons to refresh our minds regarding what we've learned.

Under the anointing of the Holy Spirit, Paul penned a powerfully prophetic statement in Second Timothy 3:1 saying, "This know also, that in the last days perilous times shall come." When we incorporate the original Greek meaning into this verse, the *Renner Interpretive Version* (*RIV*) reads:

> **You emphatically and categorically need to know with unquestionable certainty that in the very end of days — when time has sailed to its last port and no more time remains for the journey — that last season will stand in the midst of uncontrollable, unpredictable, hurtful, treacherous, and menacing times that will be emotionally difficult for people to bear.**

Once Paul made this opening statement, he began to list numerous signs that we would see manifesting in society at the very end of the age. For example, in verses 4 and 5, he lets us know that people will be "traitors, heady, highminded, lovers of pleasures more than lovers of God; having a form of godliness, but denying the power thereof: from such turn away…" (2 Timothy 3:4,5).

When we insert the original Greek meaning into these verses, here is how the *Renner Interpretive Version* (*RIV*) of Second Timothy 3:4,5 reads:

> **People will find it easy to walk away from commitments and to easily throw away relationships. They will become reckless, impulsive, and known for their enjoyment of violence. They will become full of pride and inflated with a sense of their own self-importance — to the extent that it may end up feeling like society is being hit by a typhoon; however, those menacing winds of change will eventually blow out like a storm that comes and goes. People will become fixated on the unobtainable pursuit of happiness and pleasure even more than they love God.**
>
> **Although they may possess an outward form of religiosity, they will rebuff, refute, refuse, and reject the authentic power that goes along with genuine godliness. I urgently tell you to**

mentally, spiritually, and physically turn away from and remove yourselves from such people.

Continuing his description of society in the last of the last days, Paul said, "For of this sort are they which creep into houses, and lead captive silly women laden with sins, led away with divers lusts, ever learning, and never able to come to the knowledge of the truth" (2 Timothy 3:6,7).

Taking into account the original Greek meaning, here is the *Renner Interpretive Version* (*RIV*) of Second Timothy 3:6,7:

> These sorts of people project themselves as "help" with the intention of gaining access into people's homes to manipulate them — especially women who feel overwhelmed by frustrations and disappointing failures in life whom the manipulators find easier to influence because they have so many unmet longings.
>
> These women are endlessly doing their very best to gain insight needed to help them navigate life, but they are perpetually unable to come to right conclusions based on truth.

From here, Paul went on to give his readers a concrete example from Scripture of those who had a "form of godliness but denied the power thereof." In a masterful way, he drew on an instance from Old Testament history regarding two well-known enemies of God and shared how what they did would be repeated by people living at the end of the age.

Who Were Jannes and Jambres?

In Second Timothy 3:8, Paul wrote, "Now as Jannes and Jambres withstood Moses, so do these also resist the truth: men of corrupt minds, reprobate concerning the faith." Before we unpack the meaning of this passage, we need to first establish who Jannes and Jambres are. Thankfully, because of the work of Jewish intellectuals who lived in the ancient city of Alexandria, Egypt, we have explicit historical information of who these individuals were.

First, by studying Egypt's ancient historical records, they identified that Jannes and Jambres were very influential, celebrity-type spiritual leaders in ancient Egypt. Specifically, they were the primary sorcerers, or magicians, who "withstood" Moses when he demanded that Pharaoh let the children of Israel go free (*see* Exodus 7:11, 22; 8:6,7).

In fact, Jannes and Jambres were so well known in the ancient world that even Pliny the Elder wrote about them. The historian Eusebius also wrote about these two men. Likewise, the theologian Origen wrote about them, and in addition to these sources, the names Jannes and Jambres appeared frequently in other Jewish, Christian, and pagan sources in Arabic, Aramaic, Greek, Hebrew, Latin, Old and Middle English, and Syriac.

They 'Withstood' Moses

Again, Paul wrote that "…Jannes and Jambres *withstood* Moses…" (2 Timothy 3:8). The word "withstood" is a compound of the Greek words *anti* and *histemi*. The word *anti* means *against*, and the word *histemi* means *to stand*. When compounded to form *anthistemi*, it means *to stand against* or *to stand in opposition to*. It demonstrates *the attitude of one who is fiercely opposed to something, and therefore determines to do everything within his power to resist it, to stand against it, to withstand it*, or *to defy it*.

If you study what happened at the time of Israel's exodus from Egypt (*see* Exodus 7-9), you'll see that this precisely describes how Jannes and Jambres acted. Nothing they did was accidental. Every form of resistance was strategically orchestrated through their "corrupt minds," which we will talk more about in a moment.

Interestingly, when Paul said, "Now as Jannes and Jambres withstood Moses," the word "as" is a translation of the Greek words *hon tropon*, which means *in the very same way*. And the word "now" is the Greek word *de*, which means *emphatically* or *categorically*. It serves to intensify Paul's statement, which taken together is the equivalent of his saying, *"Emphatically, in the exact same way Jannes and Jambres defiantly stood against and fiercely opposed Moses…."*

Then Paul added, "…So do these also resist the truth: men of corrupt minds, reprobate concerning the faith" (2 Timothy 3:8). The phrase "so also" is a translation of the Greek words *houtos kai*, which means *accordingly* or *in the very same way; also*. Thus, *in the exact same way*, these "spiritual mannequins" will *resist* the truth, and the word "resist" is the same Greek word *anthistemi*, which means they will *defiantly oppose and fiercely stand against* the truth.

Their 'Minds' Were 'Corrupt'

What is causing these evil, end-time influencers to defiantly oppose the truth? Paul said they have "corrupt minds" (*see* 2 Timothy 3:8). In Greek, the word "minds" is the word *nous*, and it describes *a mind marvelously created by God with the ability to think, reason, understand*, or *to comprehend*; it is *the place from which one rules and controls his inward and outward environment*. Without question, the mind is the central control center of a person's life — the place where reasoning, perception, and understanding take place. In this verse, however, the minds being referred to have become "corrupt."

This word "corrupt" is the Greek word *kataphtheiro*, which is a very strange word used only once in the entire New Testament. It is from the word *kata*, meaning *down*, and the word *phtheiro*, which describes *corruption, degeneration*, or *deterioration*. Hence, the word *kataphtheiro* — translated here as "corrupt" — means *to move downward into a state of collapse, deterioration, and ruin*. It depicts something in the process of degeneration and decay. Because these men are believing lies and teaching false doctrine, their minds, which were marvelously created by God, will progressively begin to worsen, moving downward into a state of degeneration and deterioration.

By using Jannes and Jambres' example, the Holy Spirit is telling us that at the very end of the age, spiritual leaders in the Church will become "corrupt" in their minds. In other words, people who once preached the Word of God will drift away from the truth and actually recant or reverse what they once taught. Even worse, they will defiantly stand against the Word and oppose those who teach it.

They Became 'Reprobate'

Paul went on to say these evil men will be "...reprobate concerning the faith" (2 Timothy 3:8). The word "reprobate" is the Greek word *adokimos*, and it is derived from the word *dokimos*, which means *acceptable, reliable*, or *trustworthy*. However, because an "a" has been attached to the front of the word, the meaning has been cancelled or reversed. Hence, *adokimos* means *unacceptable, unreliable*, or *unfit*. It describes *anything rejected due to its flawed nature*.

In this verse, it depicts *a mind that has become unfit and defective and no longer operating as God intended*. This can refer to *the mind of an individual* or *the mind of society that has become ill-affected from long-term exposure to negative spiritual influences — especially regarding conclusions about moral issues.* A reprobate mind eventually produces reprobate behaviors; it is *defective* or *malfunctioning*.

Paul used this word *adokimos* to not only describe the character of Jannes and Jambres, but also to describe the character of the end-time apostate leaders in the Church. Even though God gave these leaders marvelous brains, by believing and embracing wrong, negative, ungodly information for a long time, their minds will become tarnished, tainted, and ill-affected, no longer functioning correctly.

To be clear, a mind that is "reprobate" (*adokimos*) is one that has been seriously damaged by long-term, continuous exposure to evil influences and by a continual bombardment of wrong thoughts. Whether this is occurring individually or is the collective mind of society, the mind that is *reprobate* has become so *tarnished, tainted, hardened,* and both *spiritually* and *mentally compromised* that it loses its ability to arrive at sensible, godly conclusions.

That same mind may remain brilliant in many aspects, and the person who possesses that mind may be marvelously talented. Nevertheless, if that person's mind has become reprobate, it is now morally debased, unfit, and twisted in its thinking. From God's perspective, such a person — or an entire society — has lost the ability to think correctly, to separate good from evil, or to judge what is right and wrong.

We're living in a day when people's minds are being inundated with false information on the Internet and airwaves. As it stealthily creeps into people's houses through various sources, we are witnessing a last-days attack of seducing spirits bent on modifying the collective mind of society and creating a way of thinking that is free of moral restraint.

This modification process of society is spreading its tentacles into every sphere of humanity. Even people who grew up in church are now becoming ill-affected because their minds have been inundated with wrong information. That's why you need to be very careful and pray about where you send your kids to school and to college. You also need to regularly be aware of what they're listening to on their devices.

'Concerning the Faith'

Please note that the evil influencers Paul is describing in Second Timothy 3:8 became reprobate "concerning the faith." In Greek, the phrase "the faith" is *ten pistin*. It has a definite article and refers to *"THE" faith*, *"THE" doctrine*, or *"THE" non-negotiable tenets of the Christian faith*. This is not faith for miracles or faith for finances or faith for healing.

Today, we see that many of the old traditional churches do remain scripturally accurate in their creeds and church documents. Yet, while they have the right tenets of faith on paper, in their practice, some have departed from the clear, non-negotiable doctrines of Scripture and have begun to embrace practices that are forbidden by the Word of God. These churches and denominations do this in an attempt to be loving, but consequently, they embrace and condone what is clearly defined in the Bible as sin — which is very *unloving*. They are doing the lost a disservice by accepting — and sometimes *celebrating* — sin rather than teaching and warning people of the dire consequences of the path they've chosen.

Friend, we are seeing this drift from the standard of God's Word. In the Church today, there are leaders just like Jannes and Jambres who have been regularly exposed to toxic environments and wrong types of thinking to the extent that their minds are reprobate, and now they are defiantly and fiercely standing against the truth of Scripture they once preached.

Putting the Greek meanings of all these words together, here is the *Renner Interpretive Version* (*RIV*) of Second Timothy 3:8:

> **Now as Jannes and Jambres fiercely opposed and defied Moses, these also will be fiercely opposed to and will defy the truths of Scripture; they will be men with minds that have been ruined — defective, malfunctioning, and reprobate concerning the teachings of Scripture.**

This verse serves as a major alarm to our end-time generation: The Church is under an attack that is unlike any assault it has ever experienced. The remedy to this calamity is to stay intimately connected with the Lord! There is no substitute for the truth of God's Word and the empowering presence of His Holy Spirit.

Questions and Answers With Rick Renner

In the program, Rick answered the following question from one of our viewers.

Q. Who is the "elect lady" in Second John 1?

A. In Second John 1, the apostle John said he was writing "...unto the elect lady and her children, whom I love in the truth; and not I only, but also all they that have known the truth."

Some have suggested that the "elect lady" that John was addressing was the virgin Mary, but it couldn't have been Mary because at the time of this writing, she had already died. The real clue to understanding who she was can be found by doing a study of history. During that era, principal cities and Roman provinces were called "elect ladies."

When John wrote this letter, the principal city of Asia where John lived was the city of Pergamum, and Pergamum was referred to as *the elect lady*. Thus, it is likely that when John addressed the "elect lady" in verse 1 of his second letter, he was referring to the church in Pergamum, rather than to an actual woman. Therefore, Second John was an epistle to the church in Pergamum.

STUDY QUESTIONS

> Study to shew thyself approved unto God, a workman that needeth not to be ashamed, rightly dividing the word of truth.
> — 2 Timothy 2:15

1. What new facts did you learn about Jannes and Jambres from the Old Testament? What connections can you see between them and the apostate leaders that the Holy Spirit prophesied would emerge on the scene in the last days?
2. Your mind is the *central control center* of your life. Proverbs 23:7 declares, "As he thinketh in his heart, so is he...." Carefully reflect on Romans 8:5-7 and identify the differences between the "mind of the flesh" and the "mind of the Spirit." Which one do you seem to operate in more regularly?
3. The Bible has much to say about the mind and its need for God's Word. Take some time to look up each of the passages below and

identify God's instructions to you concerning the daily care of your mind. Be sure to write down anything the Holy Spirit personally speaks to you in the process.

- **Joshua 1:8**
- **Psalm 1:1-3**
- **Romans 12:2**
- **1 Corinthians 2:16**
- **Ephesians 4:22-24**
- **Colossians 3:1,2**

PRACTICAL APPLICATION

> But be ye doers of the word, and not hearers only, deceiving your own selves.
> —James 1:22

1. There are several denominational churches today that have the right tenets of faith on paper, but in their practice, they have departed from the clear, non-negotiable doctrines of Scripture. What's most alarming is that they have begun to embrace practices that are forbidden by the Word of God. What real-life examples of this *reprobate* thinking have you seen or heard? What unbiblical behavior is being tolerated — and even celebrated?
2. Why is accepting and being inclusive of unbiblical lifestyles and practices *not loving*?
3. When the disciples asked Jesus for the sign of His coming and the end of the age, the first thing He told them was to *guard themselves against deception* (*see* Matthew 24:3,4). Clearly, deception is running rampant in these last of the last days. Think for a moment. What words of wisdom might you offer to a cherished friend or family member to help that person guard his or her heart and mind from being deceived and becoming reprobate concerning the faith? Are you following this counsel yourself?

LESSON 14

TOPIC
A Hidden Prophecy!

SCRIPTURES
1. **2 Timothy 3:1** — This know also, that in the last days perilous times shall come.
2. **2 Timothy 3:8, 9, 13** — Now as Jannes and Jambres withstood Moses, so do these also resist the truth: men of corrupt minds, reprobate concerning the faith. But they shall proceed no further: for their folly shall be manifest unto all men, as theirs also was. But evil men and seducers shall wax worse and worse, deceiving, and being deceived.

GREEK WORDS
1. "withstood" — ἀνθίστημι (*anthistemi*): to stand against; to stand in opposition; it demonstrates the attitude of one who is fiercely opposed to something and therefore determines to do everything within his power to resist it; to stand against it; to withstand; to defy
2. "resist" — ἀνθίστημι (*anthistemi*): to stand against; to stand in opposition; it demonstrates the attitude of one who is fiercely opposed to something and therefore determines to do everything within his power to resist it; to stand against it; to withstand; to defy
3. "corrupt" — καταφθείρω (*kataphtheiro*): from κατά (*kata*) and φθείρω (*phtheiro*); the word κατά (*kata*) means down; the word φθείρω (*phtheiro*) means corruption, degeneration, or deterioration; hence, to move downward into a state of collapse, deterioration, and ruin; only used in 2 Timothy 3:8
4. "minds" — νοῦς (*nous*): plural, minds; the ability to think, reason, understand, or to comprehend; the place from which one rules and controls his inward and outward environment; the central control center for a human being; the place where reasoning, perception, and understanding takes place
5. "reprobate" — ἀδόκιμος (*adokimos*): unfit; rejected; anything rejected due to its flawed nature; depicts a mind that has become unfit and defective; the mind of an individual or the mind of society that has

become ill-affected, especially in regard to conclusions about moral issues; a reprobate mind eventually produces reprobate behaviors; defective; malfunctioning

6. "the faith" — τὴν πίστιν (*ten pistin*): with a definite article, "the" faith; "the" doctrine; "the" non-negotiable tenants of the Christian faith
7. "they shall proceed" — προκόπτω (*prokopto*): depicts the advancement of disease; to advance; to make progress
8. "folly" — ἄνοια (*anoia*): folly; madness; irrational thinking; brainless activity
9. "manifest" — ἔκδηλος (*ekdelos*): to point out; to make obvious; exposed; unmistakably clear
10. "evil" — πονηρός (*poneros*): plural; destruction, disaster, harm, or danger; malicious or malignant; foul, vile, hostile, and vicious; pictures not only that which is dangerous to the physical body, but also that which is dangerous to the spirit or mind
11. "seducers" — γόης (*goes*): plural; sorcerers who skillfully manipulate others; magicians; swindlers; frauds; charlatans; pretenders; pictures an imposter who poses as something he isn't for self-gain
12. "wax" — προκόπτω (*prokopto*): depicts the advancement of disease; to advance; to make progress
13. "deceiving" — πλανάω (*planao*): pictures deception; a moral wandering; one who has veered from a solid path; to be adrift; depicts a lost animal that cannot find its path; to morally lose one's bearings

SYNOPSIS

As God's people, we must be alert to the fact that Satan has launched a stealth operation to lead society off track in this final hour, loosing seducing spirits with doctrines of demons assigned to lead an entire generation into strong delusion. The enemy is using the voices of influential people in government as well as in the media and educational institutions — those who have already been beguiled and seduced to believe a lie. His goal is to victimize a last-days generation and lead them into ways of thinking and behaviors that damage their minds and steal, kill, and destroy on as many levels as possible.

This is the day in which we are living — the last of the last days that the Holy Spirit warned was coming. But He didn't reveal these things to us to scare us. He told them in advance so that we who are living at the end of the age can safeguard ourselves and those we love against these end-time developments. Despite how much influence and power these wicked and reprobate leaders have, a day will come in which God's power will ultimately devour and humiliate the power of the enemy.

The emphasis of this lesson:

Reprobate thinking will spread like gangrene in the last of the last days. Yet a time is coming when the spiritual disease the apostate leaders are spreading will be brought to a dead stop. The error of their thinking will be crystal clear to everyone, and the power of God will prove to be matchless and unbeatable in the face of evil.

A Quick Review of Our Anchor Verse

Second Timothy 3:1 is the foundational passage that sets the stage for the entire chapter. Here, under the supernatural unction of the Holy Spirit, the apostle Paul wrote, "This know also, that in the last days perilous times shall come." Once more, here is the *Renner Interpretive Version* (*RIV*) of Second Timohty 3:1:

> **You emphatically and categorically need to know with unquestionable certainty that in the very end of days — when time has sailed to its last port and no more time remains for the journey — that last season will stand in the midst of uncontrollable, unpredictable, hurtful, treacherous, and menacing times that will be emotionally difficult for people to bear.**

People in Society and the Church Will Become 'Reprobate' at the End of the Age

In our last lesson, we examined Paul's words in Second Timothy 3:8, where he said, "Now as Jannes and Jambres withstood Moses, so do these also resist the truth: men of corrupt minds, reprobate concerning the faith." In this verse, Paul was talking about leaders — both in society and in the Church — that will go astray at the end of the age and will become reprobate concerning the faith. Here is a review of the meaning of the key words and phrases in this passage:

"Now as" – These are the opening words of Second Timothy 3:8, which in Greek are *hon tropon de*. The words *hon tropon* mean *in the very same way,* and the word *de* — translated as the word "now" — is the Greek word that means *emphatically* or *categorically*. It serves to intensify Paul's statement and is the equivalent of him saying, *"Can you believe it! In the very same way Jannes and Jambres withstood Moses...."*

"Jannes and Jambres" – According to Jewish scholars living in the city of Alexandria, Egypt who had access to Egypt's historical records, Jannes and Jambres were the two leading sorcerers spoken of in the book of Exodus who withstood Moses at the time of Israel's deliverance.

"Withstood" – In Greek, the word "withstood" is a compound of the words *anti* and *histemi*. The word *anti* means *against*, and the word *histemi* means *to stand*. When they are joined to form *anthistemi*, it means *to stand against* or *to stand in opposition to*. It demonstrates *the attitude of one who is fiercely opposed to something, and therefore determines to do everything within his power to resist it, to stand against it, to withstand it*, or *to defy it*.

"So do these also resist" – The words "so also" are a translation of the Greek words *houtos kai*, which means *accordingly* or *in the very same way; also*. Thus, *in the exact same way*, these evil, end-time influencers will *resist* the truth just as Jannes and Jambres did. This word "resist" is the same Greek word *anthistemi*, which means these apostate leaders will *defiantly oppose and fiercely stand against* the truth.

"Men of corrupt minds" – The reason these apostate leaders are fighting against the truth is because they have "corrupt minds." The Greek word for "minds" is *nous*, and it describes *a mind marvelously created by God with the ability to think, reason, understand, or to comprehend*. In this case, the minds being referred to have become "corrupt." This is the strange Greek word *kataphtheiro*, a compound of the word *kata*, meaning *down*, and the word *phtheiro*, which describes *corruption, degeneration*, or *deterioration*. Hence, when a person's mind has become "corrupt" (*kataphtheiro*), it means that their mind has *progressively moved downward into a state of collapse, deterioration, and ruin*.

Inherent in the word "corrupt" (*kataphtheiro*) is the fact that these individuals were once at a high position, but they left it and began to decline (*kata*), which is a picture of what happens when a person leaves the Word of God. Anyone who takes a stand against the truth contained in the Bible and begins to go in another direction enters a state of deterioration and decay. They may call themselves progressive, but the truth is, they are *regressive* and *devolving* from what they once were.

"Reprobate concerning the faith" – Minds that progressively become corrupt eventually become "reprobate." In Greek, the word "reprobate" is *adokimoi*, which is the plural form of *adokimos* and is taken from the word *dokimos*. *Dokimos* means *approved, trustworthy, reliable,* or *fit,* but when an "a" is attached to the front of it, the meaning is cancelled. Hence, the word *adokimos* — translated here as "reprobate" — means *unapproved, untrustworthy, unreliable,* or *unfit*.

A "reprobate mind" depicts *a mind that has become unfit and defective.* In this case, the mind of an individual or the mind of society has become ill-affected, especially regarding conclusions about moral issues. In fact, Second Timothy 3:8 says these people are reprobate "concerning the faith." In Greek, the phrase "the faith" is *ten pistin,* and because it's with a definite article, it refers to "the" faith; "the" doctrine; or "the" non-negotiable tenets of the Christian faith.

Taking into account the original Greek meaning of this verse, here is the *Renner Interpretive Version (RIV)* of Second Timothy 3:8:

> **Now as Jannes and Jambres fiercely opposed and defied Moses, these also will be fiercely opposed to and will defy the truths of Scripture; they will be men with minds that have been ruined — defective, malfunctioning, and reprobate concerning the teachings of Scripture.**

This is the destructive track that much of the Church is on as man's natural reasoning strives to reach a generation that is unfamiliar with the Bible and views the standards of Scripture as too restrictive and outdated. Sadly, this is the *departure from Scripture* (THE faith) that Paul was referring to in Second Timothy 3:8.

Reprobate Thinking Will Spread Like a Spiritual Disease

The apostle Paul went on to say, "They shall proceed no further: for their folly shall be manifest unto all men, as theirs also was" (2 Timothy 3:9). The phrase "they shall proceed" is from the Greek word *prokopto,* and it means *to advance* or *to make progress.* Interestingly, it is the word used to depict *the advancement of disease throughout the body — a disease such as gangrene or cancer.* By using this word, Paul was telling us that what these reprobate leaders teach is like gangrene or cancer, and if nothing is done to stop it, it will spread to the entire Body of Christ.

Although a spiritual leader who is infected with false doctrine is only one person, he has influence in the lives of many others, and it is likely that others will be contaminated through his diseased influence. If correction doesn't come to the errant leader's life, his words and teachings have the potential to become "food" that makes others sick — especially those who are close to him.

It is interesting that Paul said the "spiritual disease" of these apostate leaders would progress no further because "…their folly shall be manifest unto all men…" (2 Timothy 3:9). The word "folly" is the Greek word *anoia*, which comes from the Greek word *nous* — the word for the *mind*. But because an "a" is attached to the front of it, its meaning is cancelled. Thus, the word *anoia* — translated here as "folly" — describes *folly*; *madness*; *irrational thinking*; or *brainless activity*.

That is what happens when people adopt false teaching that is unbiblical. They can no longer think logically or rationally. The error begins to corrupt their minds, bringing them further and further downward into decay and deterioration. A person who is embracing doctrines of demons and seducing spirits will progressively get worse and worse, and his *brainless* thinking and actions "shall be manifest unto all men" (*see* 2 Timothy 3:9).

The word "manifest" here is the Greek word *ekdelos*, which means *to point out* or *to make obvious*; *something unmistakably clear*. Eventually, the mindlessness and sheer lunacy (*anoia*) of these apostate leaders will grow out of control and be unmistakably obvious "unto all men," which in Greek means *absolutely everyone*.

A Final Showdown at the End of the Age

Take note that Paul said these degenerative individuals' folly shall be manifest unto all men, "…as theirs also was" (2 Timothy 3:9). This last phrase refers to Jannes and Jambres that Paul talked about in verse 8. The Greek word for "as" is *hos*, and it means *exactly as*. Paul was saying that *exactly as* Jannes and Jambres' power was revealed to be inferior in everyone's eyes, a moment will come when God's divine power will reveal that the apostate leaders are peddling ungodly nonsense.

Paul told us that Jannes and Jambres *resisted, stood against, withstood*, and *defied* God's power. And just as these two sorcerers *withstood* Moses, Paul said at the end of the age there would be well-known personalities — religious, social, and political — who would emerge on the scene to oppose the Gospel and present an alternative message. It will be part of an end-time, worldwide mutiny against God that Paul prophesied about in Second Thessalonians 2:3.

The Scripture makes it clear that this last-days development *will* occur. But Paul said that just as Pharaoh's sorcerers were unable to compete with the power of God, so, too, these end-time wanderers will be unable to compete with His mighty power. Herein is a prophecy of a final showdown at the end of the age — one in which the power of God will prove to be unbeatable in the face of evil.

Just as God's power worked through Moses to confront the powers of evil in his day, that same divine power will flow mightily through a remnant of believers in the last-days Church. And as God's power is made manifest, the brainlessness of warped ideologies and last-days doctrinal nonsense will become evident for all to see. God's power will ultimately devour and humiliate the power of the enemy.

'Evil Men and Seducers Shall Wax Worse and Worse'

To be clear, Paul declared that before this great end-time display of God's power takes place, the activities of evil men — those with a form of godliness but who deny the power of it — will spin further and further out of control as time passes. In Second Timothy 3:13, he wrote, "But evil men and seducers shall wax worse and worse, deceiving, and being deceived."

The phrase "evil men" in Greek is from the words *poneroi anthrapoi*, which are both plural. The word *anthrapoi* describes *mankind at large*, and the word *poneroi* is from the word *poneros*, which describes *destruction, disaster, harm*, or *danger*. It depicts *something malicious or malignant*; something *foul, vile, hostile, and vicious*. Moreover, it shows not only that which is dangerous to the physical body, but also that which is dangerous to the spirit or mind.

Make no mistake. The alternative messages that these leaders are propagating as "help" are *foul, vile*, and *malignant*. That fact that these words are in plural form tells us this will be a widespread issue throughout society and in the Church at the end of the age.

Paul said, "Evil men *and* seducers…" (2 Timothy 3:13). The word "and" is the Greek word *de*, and it serves as an exclamation marker. Paul used it here to reach through the pages of Scripture and grab our attention. Along with a plethora of vile, wicked men, there will also be "seducers," which is the Greek word *goes*. It is plural and describes *sorcerers who skillfully manipulate others*. It can also refer to *magicians, swindlers, frauds, charlatans,* or *pretenders*. This word pictures *an imposter who poses as something he isn't for self-gain*. Seeking to be popular and obtain a following, they use their position to cast a spell on people and pull them under their influence.

These misguided, manipulating, deceiving influencers will "wax worse and worse" (*see* 2 Timothy 3:13). The word "wax" here is from the Greek word *prokopto*, which is the same word translated as "they shall proceed" in verse 9. Again, it depicts *the advancement of disease*, and Paul uses this word to alert us to the fact that what these evil influencers are teaching is like cancer or gangrene spreading through society and the Church.

This lets us know that the apostate Church will become sicker and sicker, going from bad to worse — "deceiving and being deceived." Interestingly, both "deceiving" and "deceived" are a translation of the Greek word *planao*, which pictures *deception* or *a moral wandering*. It depicts *one who has veered from a solid path and is now teetering on the edge of a dangerous cliff*. This same word was used to describe *a lost animal that couldn't find its way back home*.

Get the picture: These end-time false teachers are going to go about luring people off the solid path of Scripture. In fact, they will draw people so far off track that unless someone reaches out to help them, the deceived ones won't be able to find their way back to the truth. These seducers will become so morally bankrupt they will believe their own lies, thereby deceiving themselves and morally losing their bearings. The poison they've been feeding others is what they've also been eating themselves. It's no wonder their minds have become corrupted and they're reprobate concerning the faith.

Factoring in all that we've examined, here is the Renner Interpretive Version (*RIV*) of Second Timothy 3:8, 9, and 13:

Now as Jannes and Jambres fiercely opposed and defied Moses, these also will be fiercely opposed to and will defy the truths of

Scripture; they will be men with minds that have been ruined — defective, malfunctioning, and reprobate concerning the teachings of Scripture.

But the advance of spiritual disease they spread will be halted, and their irrational way of thinking — their lunacy, madness, and spiritual nonsense — will become unmistakably clear to all men, as theirs also was....

But these wicked men — real, bona fide frauds who masquerade as spiritual leaders — will lead people off track as they spread their deadly teachings and put people under their magic spell. Over time, they will go from bad to worse, deceiving and being self-deceived by the nonsense they communicate to others.

Friend, God has called us to speak clearly and authoritatively from His Word, holding tightly to what the *Scripture* says, not what the end-time society says. To avoid being taken captive by the infectious deceptions these pretenders are peddling, keep your mind renewed daily with the Word of God, stay connected in a vibrant, on-fire church that accurately teaches the Scriptures, and stay filled with the Holy Spirit.

Questions and Answers With Rick Renner

In the program, Rick answered the following question from one of our viewers.

Q. What is meant by Paul's statement: "Satan is the god of this world"?

A. In Second Corinthians 4:4, the apostle Paul identified Satan as "the god of this world." The key to understanding this is in knowing the meaning of the word "world." It is the Greek word *kosmos*, which doesn't describe the physical planet or the universe, rather, it describes *the ordered systems of the world*. These would include the systems of education, entertainment, government, fashion, and the courts.

When Paul said that Satan is the "god of this world," he was actually informing us that Satan exercises his influence through all the world systems. If we look at our culture, it is clear that the devil is definitely working through the entertainment industry, the education system, the government, and the legal system. Our enemy animates and manipulates those in his control like puppets in the hands of a masterful puppeteer, speaking through all these world systems to exercise his authority and power. That is what is meant by Satan being the god of this world.

STUDY QUESTIONS

> Study to shew thyself approved unto God, a workman that
> needeth not to be ashamed, rightly dividing the word of truth.
> — 2 Timothy 2:15

1. In this lesson, we learned that to avoid being taken captive by the infectious deceptions of apostate leaders, we must keep our mind renewed daily with God's Word (*see* Romans 12:2); stay connected in a vibrant, on-fire church that accurately teaches the Scriptures (*see* Hebrews 10:24,25); and stay filled with the Holy Spirit (*see* Ephesians 5:18). Are you actively pursuing these three practices? In which one(s) do you know you need to come up higher?
2. Just as Pharaoh's sorcerers were unable to compete with God's mighty power, neither will the end-time, apostate leaders be unable to stand against Him. Indeed, the One we serve is the **Almighty God**, which is a name that appears multiple times in Scripture. Check out these verses declaring God's omnipotence. How do these verses infuse you with fresh faith in God's ability? *See* Job 42:4; Psalm 115:3; 135:6; Matthew 19:26; Luke 1:37; Ephesians 3:20.
3. What does Jude 23 say we are to do for those who are in error and heading in the wrong direction? (Consider the example provided in Genesis 19:15-17.) According to First Timothy 2:1-4, what is the greatest and most impactful way we can obey this instruction? Are you doing this?

PRACTICAL APPLICATION

> But be ye doers of the word, and not hearers only,
> deceiving your own selves.
> — James 1:22

1. When you think of people who have refused to budge from the rock-solid, non-negotiable teachings of Scripture, who comes to mind? What stands out and shines brightest about their life? Why not take some time to pray for their continued strength to hold unswervingly to the truth in all they do and say.

2. On the flipside, who comes to mind when you think of those whose minds have become *corrupted* over time? How have they veered away from God's Word? What alternative "truths" are they holding on to and offering to others? (These people could be spiritual leaders, fellow church members, friends, family members, or coworkers.)

3. Now, more than ever, you need to be connected to people who are rooted in God's Word and whose sense of discernment is trustworthy. With that in mind, ask yourself:
   - *Do I have God-fearing, Scripture-following people in my life?*
   - *Am I a member of a church that is grounded in God's Word and is a safe haven for me?*
   - *Do I trust the spiritual leadership of my pastor or spiritual leader?*

4. If you didn't answer a solid *yes* to those questions, ask yourself, *Why am I still going to a church that I don't feel is safe, and why am I sitting under leaders I feel I can't trust?* Take time to pray and ask the Lord how He would have you address this.

LESSON 15

TOPIC
How To Navigate an End-Times Storm

SCRIPTURES

1. **2 Timothy 3:1** — This know also, that in the last days perilous times shall come.

2. **2 Timothy 3:14-17** — But continue thou in the things which thou hast learned and hast been assured of, knowing of whom thou hast learned them; and that from a child thou hast known the holy scriptures, which are able to make thee wise unto salvation through faith which is in Christ Jesus. All scripture is given by inspiration of God, and is profitable for doctrine, for reproof, for correction, for instruction in righteousness: that the man of God may be perfect, thoroughly furnished unto all good works.

GREEK WORDS

1. "continue" — μένω (*meno*): to stay, remain, or abide; to firmly endure; to continue steadfastly; to be unwavering; to be unmoving; a resolute decision to remain steadfast to a location or principle; to hold one's ground to the point of fighting back; portrays something that lasts, persists, or endures
2. "from" — ἀπό (*apo*): from; pointing to a very early moment
3. "child" — βρέφος (*brephos*): an infant or newborn below the age of a toddler
4. "able" — δύναμις (*dunamis*): able; power; pictures explosive, superhuman power that comes with enormous energy and produces phenomenal, extraordinary, and unparalleled results
5. "wise" — σοφός (*sophos*): depicts wisdom not naturally attained; special insight; used to describe those who are brilliant, intellectually sharp, or especially enlightened; a class of individuals whom the world would call clever, astute, smart, or intellectually brilliant; term reserved for those considered to be intellectually impressive that were a cut above the rest of society
6. "salvation" — σωτηρία (*soteria*): deliverance; salvation; conveys the ideas of *salvation and wholeness* in every part of life; a state of deliverance, healing, and wholeness; to protect, keep safe, or keep under protection
7. "reproof" — ἔλεγχος (*elegchos*): to expose, convict, or cross-examine for the purpose of conviction, as when convicting a lawbreaker in a court of law; the image of a lawyer who brings evidence that is indisputable and undeniable so that the accused person's actions are irrefutably brought to light and the offender is exposed and convicted; used to denote a lawyer who worked to convince people of a new way of thinking or a new way of seeing things

SYNOPSIS

The cure for the craziness, the solution for the insanity, and the remedy for the reprobate is God's Word. Nothing in this world is more precious and priceless! **Hebrews 4:12** (*AMPC*) says:

> **For the Word that God speaks is alive and full of power [making it active, operative, energizing, and effective]; it is sharper**

than any two-edged sword, penetrating to the dividing line of
the breath of life (soul) and [the immortal] spirit, and of joints
and marrow [of the deepest parts of our nature], exposing
and sifting and analyzing and judging the very thoughts and
purposes of the heart.

Now more than ever, the Church, the world, and *you* need the Word of God! The Word packs the power to save your soul, incinerate lies, and crush stubborn habits and hangups that are rooted in wrong thinking. The way to navigate these stormy end times is to grab hold of the Word with all your might, hold it tight, and never let it out of your sight!

The emphasis of this lesson:

To successfully navigate the end-time storms, God has given us the timeless truth of Scripture. As you take it in and hold steadfastly to it, it will bring you face to face with solid teaching, healthy conviction, spiritual maturity, and "stand-up-again" power! It will completely equip you to thrive and go the distance in these last days in which we live.

A Final Recap of Our Anchor Verse

In Second Timothy 3:1, the Holy Spirit spoke through Paul and delivered this urgent message to all believers of all generations: "This know also, that in the last days perilous times shall come." For a final time, let's quickly review the *Renner Interpretive Version* (*RIV*) of Second Timothy 3:1:

> You emphatically and categorically need to know with unquestionable certainty that in the very end of days — when time has sailed to its last port and no more time remains for the journey — that last season will stand in the midst of uncontrollable, unpredictable, hurtful, treacherous, and menacing times that will be emotionally difficult for people to bear.

As dismal as this may sound, we don't have to despair. God has given us everything we need to live godly and to successfully sail through this end-time season (*see* 2 Peter 1:3). As we grab hold of His Word and receive the empowerment of His Spirit, we can learn to thrive and even help others make it through these perilous times.

'Continue' in What Is Right

We have seen in our last few lessons that at the very end of the age, many notable leaders in society and in the Church will veer off course, walking away from the solid path of Scripture and embracing deep deception and perverted thinking. At the same time, they will lure many away from the truth and onto the same reprobate road they are traveling.

To equip God's people so that they're not sucked into the insanity that is proliferating in society, Paul wrote Second Timothy 3:14-17 — a time-tested remedy for remaining strong in these last of the last days.

He began by saying, "But continue thou in the things which thou hast learned and hast been assured of, knowing of whom thou hast learned them" (2 Timothy 3:14). This instruction is extremely vital. When Paul said "continue," he used the Greek word *meno*, which means *to stay*, *remain*, or *abide*. It can also be translated *to firmly endure*; *to continue steadfastly*; *to be unwavering*; or *to be unmoving*. It is *a resolute decision to remain steadfast to a location or principle* and it carries the idea of *holding one's ground to the point of fighting back*. This word *meno* portrays something that *lasts*, *persists*, or *endures*.

Considering all this meaning, Paul was telling Timothy — and *us* — "Refuse to budge, hold your ground, do not flinch, and do not move from the things you have learned and have been assured of. Stick with the principles of God's Word, and you won't drift off course in this age when so many people are drifting."

The Scriptures Provide You With Everything You Need

We know for certain that in Second Timothy 3:14, Paul is talking about holding on to God's Word because of what he says in the very next verse: "And that from a child thou hast known the holy scriptures, which are able to make thee wise unto salvation through faith which is in Christ Jesus" (2 Timothy 3:15). There are several important words in this passage you need to know.

First is the word "from" — the Greek word *apo*, which means *from*, but it is specifically pointing to an earlier moment. Paul said, "from a child," which tells us he was pointing to the early years of Timothy's life when his mother began teaching him God's Word. Interestingly, the word "child" is the Greek word *brephos*, which describes *an infant or newborn below the age of a toddler*.

Timothy began to receive the instructions of Scripture from the time he was a newborn baby. This is why I encourage people to pour the Word of God into their children or grandchildren at the earliest age you can. When you do, the truth will stay with that child into adulthood.

The word "scriptures" in verse 15 is the Greek word *grapho*, which refers to *every jot, every little tittle of the law*. This seems to indicate that Timothy had been given an appreciation for every comma, every period, and every little nuance written in the Scriptures; to him it was *all* holy. He embraced every aspect of God's Word, which is *able* to make us wise unto salvation.

The word "able" here is a form of the Greek word *dunamis*, which describes *ability* and *power*. It pictures *explosive, superhuman power that comes with enormous energy and produces phenomenal, extraordinary, and unparalleled results*. This reiterates what we read in Hebrews 4:12 — that the Word of God inherently packs power to produce supernatural results in and through our life. When you stick with the Word, power is released to make you *wise unto salvation*.

In Greek, the word "wise" is a form of the word *sophos*, which depicts *special insight* or *wisdom not naturally attained*. This term was used to describe those who are *brilliant, intellectually sharp*, or *especially enlightened — a class of individuals whom the world would call clever, astute, smart*, or *intellectually brilliant*. This term was reserved for *those considered to be intellectually impressive that were a cut above the rest of society*.

The use of this word *sophos* — translated here as "wise" — tells us that when we hold tightly to God's Word, it makes us *sharp and brilliant*, and it *gives us the upper hand*. In a world where people are becoming mindless and deteriorating morally, those who stick with the Word stand out above the crowd, and that Word brings them *salvation*.

The word "salvation" is the Greek word *soteria*, and it describes *deliverance* and *salvation*. Equally important, it conveys the ideas of *salvation and wholeness in every part of life*. It is a state of deliverance, healing, and wholeness, and it means *to protect, keep safe*, or *keep under protection*. This tells us the Word of God will give us everything we need as long as we stay in it.

Taking into account the original Greek meaning in this verse, here is the *Renner Interpretive Version* (*RIV*) of Second Timothy 3:15:

> **And from the age of an infant, you have experienced every jot and tittle of the sacred Scriptures, which are explosively powerful and can release phenomenal, extraordinary, and unparalleled results in making one wise — that is, to have wisdom not naturally attained and to become so enlightened to a delivering salvation that protects you, keeps you, and brings wholeness to you in every sphere of life.**

'All Scripture Is Given by Inspiration of God'

The apostle Paul wrapped up his prophetic forecast of the end of the age describing in detail the remedy for remaining spiritually strong and healthy. In Second Timothy 3:16 he declared: "All scripture is given by inspiration of God, and is profitable for doctrine, for reproof, for correction, for instruction in righteousness." Although this truth is a source of confidence and strength for every believer, it is especially powerful for those living in this final hour.

First, notice the word "all," which is the Greek word *pasa*. It means *all, no part excluded; every bit of it; each and every part*. This word is used to indicate *absolutely all* of Scripture. The word "scripture" is the Greek word *graphe*, and it is used 51 times in the New Testament to describe *the Old and New Testament Scriptures*. Hence, all Scripture — every part of it, nothing excluded — is given by inspiration of God.

This brings us to the phrase "inspiration of God" — the Greek word *theopneustos*. It is from the words *theos* and *pneo*. The word *theos* means *God*, and it is from where we get the word *theology*, which is the *study of God*. The word *pneo* is the term for *spirit*, and it means *to breathe*. Thus, a good translation of the first part of verse 16 is *"All Scripture is God-breathed."* But a closer look at the historical meaning of the word *pneo* in the Old Testament reveals three additional, very important meanings:

#1: The word *pneo* was the ancient word for *perfume*. If someone wanted to get rid of a bad smell in their home, they would open a jar or bottle of perfume (*pneo*) and allow that fragrance to filter through the air. This tells us the inspired Word of God is like sweet-smelling perfume. Every time you open it up, the fragrance of Heaven fills the atmosphere of your life.

#2: The word *pneo* was the word used to describe *the air that is blown from the mouth into a wind instrument to produce music.* An example of this is a flutist placing a flute to his lips, inhaling and filling his lungs with air, and then blowing the air through the flute to produce music. This is a demonstration of the word *pneo*, and this lets us know that when the noise of the world and the voice of the enemy and our flesh are screaming in our ears, if we will open God's Word, the sounds of Heaven will be released in our life.

#3: The word *pneo* was the Old-Testament word for *creative power.* This word was used in Genesis 1 to describe the Spirit of God as He moved upon the face of the deep and began to create the world through His Words. When we speak God's Word aloud over our lives, over our situations, and against the enemy, the creative power of Heaven is released.

So, when we read, "All scripture is given by inspiration of God," we see that it is literally breathed out by God Himself and it brings the fragrance of Heaven, the sounds of Heaven, and the creative power of Heaven into our lives.

Friend, when you dig into the Scriptures and release them in your life…

- you detonate creative power inside you and around you.
- you allow God, the Great Musician, to play an amazing new song in and through your life for you and others to hear.
- you release the heavenly fragrance of God into your life, which has the power to change the aroma of any "smelly" situation in your life!

All this meaning is packed within the word *pneo* — translated here as "inspiration."

All Scripture Is 'Profitable'

In addition to being "God-breathed," all Scripture "…is profitable for doctrine…" (2 Timothy 3:16). In Greek, the word for "profitable" is *ophelimos*, which means *helpful, profitable, useful, beneficial; something that is to one's advantage.* It can also be translated as *needful* or *obligatory; something that is mandatory, essential,* or *an absolute requirement.* The use of the word *ophelimos* lets us know that Scripture is *not* optional in our lives — it is *mandatory.* If we're going to release creative power, bring the sounds of Heaven, and experience God's life-changing aroma in our lives, we must have His Word.

Specifically, Paul said that all Scripture is good and beneficial *for* doctrine, *for* reproof, *for* correction, and *for* instruction in righteousness. What's interesting is that the word "for" appears four times, and it is the Greek word *pros*, which describes *an intimately close, face-to-face encounter*.

The Scriptures are profitable for "doctrine." The word "doctrine" is the Greek word *didaskalia*, which describes *well-packaged teaching that applies to and affects one's life*. So when Paul said that all Scripture is "for doctrine," it means "every part of the Old and New Testament brings you intimately close and face to face with excellent, high-level teaching that will change your life."

The Scriptures are profitable for "reproof." The word "reproof" is from the Greek word *elegchos*, and it means *to expose, to convict,* or *to cross-examine for the purpose of conviction, as when convicting a lawbreaker in a court of law*. It is the image of a lawyer who brings evidence that is indisputable and undeniable so that the accused person's actions are irrefutably brought to light and the offender is exposed and convicted. This word was also used to denote *a lawyer who worked to convince people of a new way of thinking or a new way of seeing things*. Thus, the Word of God has the innate ability to convict us with indisputable evidence and bring us face to face with the areas of our lives that need to change.

The Scriptures are profitable for "correction." The word "correction" is from the Greek word *epanorthosis*, which means *to correct, to set straight, to erect, to set upright,* or *cause to be level*. It describes an action that picks one up and sets him upright on his feet again after having been previously knocked down in life. This meaning is especially encouraging for people living at the end of the age. When life is harsh, harmful, and emotionally hard to bear and you've been knocked flat by disappointments and difficulties, the Word of God has "stand-again" power! If you receive and embrace the Word, it will resurrect you back to life.

The Scriptures are profitable for "instruction in righteousness." The word "instruction" here is from the Greek word *paideia*, which means *to train* or *educate a child and give him or her everything necessary to prepare for life*. It describes *child-training* or *the process of getting a child ready for adulthood so afterward he can be sent out fully equipped to successfully live as he was taught and trained to do*. This brings us to the word "righteousness," which is the Greek word *dikaiosune*, and it describes *right living*. It epitomizes those who live by a righteous standard that results in upright living.

Therefore, when you receive and embrace God's holy Word, it brings you face to face with spiritual maturity in your life.

When we insert the original Greek meaning of all these words, the *Renner Interpretive Version* (*RIV*) of Second Timothy 3:16 reads:

> **All Scripture — each and every bit of it, and not a part of it excluded — has been breathed out from the mouth of God and carries creative power, beautiful new heavenly sounds, and it is filled with a divine fragrance to change the smell in any atmosphere; it is essential for doctrine that will affect the way you live your life; it is needed to confront and convict you about areas that need to change in your life and to bring you new ways of seeing things; it sets straight and picks up those who have fallen flat in life and puts them back on their feet again; it provides instruction that is essential to live an upright life.**

The Scriptures Thoroughly Equip Us for Good Works

Paul wrapped up his teaching by informing us that God has given us the Scriptures, "That the man of God may be perfect, thoroughly furnished unto all good works" (2 Timothy 3:17). This verse is simply packed with meaning. For instance, the word "that" is the Greek word *hina*, and it means *in order that* and *points to a specific purpose*. The word "man" is from the Greek word *anthropos*, and it is a generic term for *a member of the human race, including both men and women*.

Next is the word "perfect" — the Greek word *artios*, which means *complete, mature, adequate, and completely sufficient in every way*. This word informs us that the Scriptures have *a specific purpose for each member of the human race* — every man and every woman — and that purpose includes making each of us *mature* and *completely sufficient in every way*.

The Scriptures also enable us to be "…thoroughly furnished unto all good works." The phrase "thoroughly furnished" is from the Greek word *exartidzo*, which means *to completely deck out* or *to fully supply* and *to fully equip*. It depicts *a simple ship that had previously been ill-equipped for traveling, but now has been loaded with new equipment and gear that enables it to sail anywhere*. Such boats were fully supplied, completely equipped, or thoroughly furnished.

The word *exartidzo* depicts *a boat equipped to make it through all kinds of weather, including strong storms*; it is *a boat equipped for long-distance sailing*. How fitting that Paul would choose a navigational word (*eschatos*) to begin the chapter and another (*exartidzo*) to end the chapter. God is telling us that in order to successfully sail to the very last port of time, we must be fully equipped by the Word of God.

By using this word *exartidzo*, the Holy Spirit is telling us that as we embrace and take in the Scriptures, we are fully equipped to confront any situation that comes our way. In fact, it says we are "…thoroughly furnished unto all good works." The word "all" is the Greek word *pan*, which is *all-encompassing* and refers to *everything, with nothing excluded*. The word "good" in Greek is the word *agathos*, and it describes *anything good, beneficial, or profitable; that which is brave or noble*.

And finally, the word "works" is a translation of the Greek word *ergon*, which describes *actions, deeds*, or *activities*. This word often referred to *a person's occupation, one's labor*, or *the things produced by someone's effort or life*. It could also describe *a person's line of work, his career, his occupation, his labor*, or *his profession*; it denotes *the result of hard work or hard labor*. This word is so all-encompassing that it pictures *one's belief and conduct*.

Putting the meanings of all these words together, here is the *Renner Interpretive Version* (*RIV*) of Second Timothy 3:17:

> **In order that any person belonging to God will be mature and sufficient in every way — completely outfitted with all the spiritual gear needed to equip anyone to sail long distances and through any type of spiritual storm or weather; it will enable anyone to bravely and nobly carry out all the good works that are needed to become a success in any sphere of life.**

Friend, that is what the Word of God will do in *your* life! These amazing effects were not just for the apostles and First Century believers. Nor are they just for your pastor and the missionaries serving around the world. This supernatural equipping and empowerment is for *you*, too, and you will experience it as you fully embrace the Scriptures.

So begin taking in God's Word daily and applying the blood of Jesus to your life. As you stay filled with the Spirit of God and continue to feed on His Word, Heaven only knows the great exploits you will do to advance His Kingdom and bring Him glory!

Questions and Answers With Rick Renner

In the program, Rick answered the following question from one of our viewers.

Q. What does the name "Lucifer" mean?

A. The name "Lucifer" appears in Isaiah 14 and in the Septuagint, which is the Greek version of the Old Testament, and it is a translation of the word *phosphorus*. What do you hear and think of when you read that word? That's right. It's where we get the word *phosphorus*, which is a highly reactive, poisonous, nonmetallic element of the nitrogen group. If you've ever struck a match to light a fire, the red tip that burst into a flame was made of phosphorus.

In Greek, the word *phosphorus* is a compound of two words; the word *phos*, which means *light*, and the word *pheros*, which means *to bear*. When compounded to form *phosphorus*, it is translated as the name "Lucifer," meaning *one who bears or carries light*. The reason he was called Lucifer (*phosphorous*) is because he was originally covered with every precious stone that was used to reflect God's light (*see* Ezekiel 28:13).

The Bible also says that Lucifer was the "anointed the cherub that covers" who stood in the very presence of God and served as a mirror to reflect God's glory (*see* Ezekiel 28:14,15). As the glory of God emanated from Him, it would shine on Lucifer, and all the stones that covered him would begin to refract God's light, enabling God to see and enjoy His own glory.

At some point after he was created, Lucifer wrongly began to believe *he* was generating that glorious light on his own. Pride entered his heart and he fell into deception, which is why Ezekiel 28:17 says: "Thine heart was lifted up because of thy beauty, thou hast corrupted thy wisdom by reason of thy brightness…." Lucifer forgot he was a *reflector* and he began to think he was a generator.

Now you know why he was called "Lucifer" — *phosphorous* — when he was first created.

STUDY QUESTIONS

> Study to shew thyself approved unto God, a workman that needeth not to be ashamed, rightly dividing the word of truth.
> — 2 Timothy 2:15

1. As challenging as this end-time season is, God has made special provisions for you to successfully make it through. According to these passages of Scripture, what has the Lord promised to provide for you?
   - Isaiah 50:4
   - Luke 12:11,12
   - 2 Corinthians 9:8
   - Ephesians 1:3
   - James 4:6
   - 2 Peter 1:3

2. Without question, the Word of God is packed with explosive, life-transforming power! Take some time to *meditate on the message* of these amazing verses and identify what kinds of results you can expect to see in your life as you regularly spend time reading and studying Scripture.
   - Psalm 119:9
   - Jeremiah 23:29
   - John 15:3; 17:17
   - Acts 20:32
   - Romans 1:16
   - Ephesians 5:26
   - Hebrews 4:12
   - James 1:21

PRACTICAL APPLICATION

> But be ye doers of the word, and not hearers only, deceiving your own selves.
> — James 1:22

Questions and Answers With Rick Renner

In the program, Rick answered the following question from one of our viewers.

Q. What does the name "Lucifer" mean?

A. The name "Lucifer" appears in Isaiah 14 and in the Septuagint, which is the Greek version of the Old Testament, and it is a translation of the word *phosphorus*. What do you hear and think of when you read that word? That's right. It's where we get the word *phosphorus*, which is a highly reactive, poisonous, nonmetallic element of the nitrogen group. If you've ever struck a match to light a fire, the red tip that burst into a flame was made of phosphorus.

In Greek, the word *phosphorus* is a compound of two words; the word *phos*, which means *light*, and the word *pheros*, which means *to bear*. When compounded to form *phosphorus*, it is translated as the name "Lucifer," meaning *one who bears or carries light*. The reason he was called Lucifer (*phosphorous*) is because he was originally covered with every precious stone that was used to reflect God's light (*see* Ezekiel 28:13).

The Bible also says that Lucifer was the "anointed the cherub that covers" who stood in the very presence of God and served as a mirror to reflect God's glory (*see* Ezekiel 28:14,15). As the glory of God emanated from Him, it would shine on Lucifer, and all the stones that covered him would begin to refract God's light, enabling God to see and enjoy His own glory.

At some point after he was created, Lucifer wrongly began to believe *he* was generating that glorious light on his own. Pride entered his heart and he fell into deception, which is why Ezekiel 28:17 says: "Thine heart was lifted up because of thy beauty, thou hast corrupted thy wisdom by reason of thy brightness…." Lucifer forgot he was a *reflector* and he began to think he was a generator.

Now you know why he was called "Lucifer" — *phosphorous* — when he was first created.

STUDY QUESTIONS

> Study to shew thyself approved unto God, a workman that needeth not to be ashamed, rightly dividing the word of truth.
> — 2 Timothy 2:15

1. As challenging as this end-time season is, God has made special provisions for you to successfully make it through. According to these passages of Scripture, what has the Lord promised to provide for you?
   - **Isaiah 50:4**
   - **Luke 12:11,12**
   - **2 Corinthians 9:8**
   - **Ephesians 1:3**
   - **James 4:6**
   - **2 Peter 1:3**

2. Without question, the Word of God is packed with explosive, life-transforming power! Take some time to *meditate on the message* of these amazing verses and identify what kinds of results you can expect to see in your life as you regularly spend time reading and studying Scripture.
   - **Psalm 119:9**
   - **Jeremiah 23:29**
   - **John 15:3; 17:17**
   - **Acts 20:32**
   - **Romans 1:16**
   - **Ephesians 5:26**
   - **Hebrews 4:12**
   - **James 1:21**

PRACTICAL APPLICATION

> But be ye doers of the word, and not hearers only, deceiving your own selves.
> —James 1:22

1. Looking at your own life, how would you describe the difference between when you are regularly spending time in God's Word versus when you're not regularly spending time in it? What effect does the Word have on your attitude, actions, and words? How about on your physical health, your relationships, your finances, and your overall well-being?
2. God said His Word is profitable for "correction," which means it has "stand-up" power to pick you up and set you upright on your feet again after you've been knocked down by circumstances. What example can you think of in your life when this happened? In what area of your life do you presently need God's Word to pick you up and put you back on your feet again?
3. Knowing the Bible is the ultimate remedy for successfully navigating these end times, what adjustments can you make in your life — especially regarding your leisure time — to enable you to spend more quality time feasting on the fabulous nourishment of Scripture?
4. The Holy Spirit didn't give us the prophetic end-times outlook in Second Timothy 3 to scare us. He did it to *prepare* us. How do you feel these lessons are preparing you to survive and thrive in these last days?

CLAIM YOUR FREE RESOURCE!

As a way of introducing you further to the teaching ministry of Rick Renner, we would like to send you FREE of charge his teaching, "How To Receive a Miraculous Touch From God" on CD or as an MP3 download.

In His earthly ministry, Jesus commonly healed *all* who were sick of *all* their diseases. In this profound message, learn about the manifold dimensions of Christ's wisdom, goodness, power, and love toward all humanity who came to Him in faith with their needs.

☑ YES, I want to receive Rick Renner's monthly teaching letter!

Simply scan the QR code to claim this resource or go to:
renner.org/claim-your-free-offer

WITH US!

renner.org

facebook.com/rickrenner • facebook.com/rennerdenise
youtube.com/rennerministries • youtube.com/deniserenner
instagram.com/rickrrenner • instagram.com/rennerministries_
instagram.com/rennerdenise

www.ingramcontent.com/pod-product-compliance
Lightning Source LLC
LaVergne TN
LVHW051607070426
835507LV00021B/2816